SO I'M NOT PERFECT

SO I'M NOT PERFECT
A Psychology of Humility

by

Robert J. Furey, Ph.D.

ALBA · HOUSE  NEW · YORK

SOCIETY OF ST. PAUL, 2187 VICTORY BLVD., STATEN ISLAND, NEW YORK 10314

Library of Congress Cataloging-in-Publication Data

Furey, Robert J.
  So I'm not perfect.

  *1. Humility—Psychological aspects. 2. Spiritual
life—Catholic authors. I. Title. II. Title: So I
am not perfect.*
BV4647.H8F87   1986   241'.4   86-3301
ISBN 0-8189-0499-2

---

*Designed, printed and bound in the United States of
America by the Fathers and Brothers of the
Society of St. Paul, 2187 Victory Boulevard,
Staten Island, New York 10314, as part of their
communications apostolate.*

---

5 6 7 8 9 (Current Printing: first digit)

To my wife Jane,
my children Shawn and Colleen,
and my grandmother Veronica Calby

Acknowledgments

I am indebted to the many fine people I have had the privilege of working with. So much of what I have learned from clients and colleagues finds its way into this book.

Specifically, I would like to thank Rev. Raymond McCarthy for providing me with valuable information on the theory and practice of Alcoholics Anonymous. His direction was pivotal in the development of this book.

Contents

Introduction

Promises of greatness always attract desperate audiences. Books offering advice on improving health, happiness, self-esteem, appearance and sexual prowess are in constant demand. The contemporary consumer prowls for ways to become "better." This relentless search for better has become big business. There is indeed a seeker born every minute.

Like other existential therapists, I believe there is an innate drive to actualize our potential. One of the few things we know for certain is that living organisms grow. When we resist growth, emotional and psychological problems arise. Psychological health belongs to the individual whose initiative and environment allow for human development. Nature, however, has given us so much to work with that there is not enough time in a lifetime to actualize all our potential. The best we can do is the best we can do.

This book attempts to destroy a certain myth about human growth. Too many people see growth only in terms of doing things they could not do previously. This means becoming less afraid, more assertive, more expressive or doing that extra push-up. If we can see our growth, we know we are alive. Visible changes also serve to convince others of our vitality.

This view of human growth, however, presents serious problems. Certain talents in each of us refuse to blossom.

We do not spend our lives getting better in all areas of our being. We all operate within the confines of insurmountable limitations. Yet we can grow even when imprisoned by the most severe constraints.

When an alcoholic enters Alcoholics Anonymous (A.A.) for treatment, his first task is to accept his limitations. A.A., which may be our most effective means of help for the alcoholic, introduces the drinker to a virtue rarely considered today—humility. The organization uses as its motto a prayer which beautifully articulates the growth process:

God grant me the serenity to accept the things
   I cannot change,
courage to change the things I can,
and wisdom to know the difference.

If you do not believe in God, maybe this is because you have not developed the humility it takes to look for God. Bill W., one of the co-founders of A.A. and himself an alcoholic, once said of alcoholics:

Our very first problem is to accept our present circumstances as they are, ourselves as we are, and the people about us as they are. This is to adopt a realistic humility without which no genuine advance can even begin. Again and again, we shall need to return to that unflattering point of departure. This is an exercise in acceptance that we can profitably practice every day of our lives.

Provided we strenuously avoid turning these realistic surveys of the facts of life into unrealistic alibis for apathy or defeatism, they can be the sure foundation upon which increased emotional health and therefore spiritual progress can begin.[1]

This advice can apply to all of us. Self-acceptance is the foundation of emotional health. Emotional health, in turn, begets mature spirituality.

This book will use Alcoholics Anonymous as a living example of the need for genuine human humility. More so than any of our other therapeutic approaches, A.A. addresses the human need for humility and spirituality. These dimensions are sorely lacking from our more secular therapies.

In the pages ahead I will deal with the forgotten virtue, humility. I will try to define it and explain why it remains crucial to our spiritual health and psychological well-being. Humility, however, is more than the subject of this book; it is the fuel that motivates me through every page.

Many times I've started writing best sellers. I lavished in the thought of being on top of *The New York Times* Best Seller List. But this wonderful fantasy created a tremendous writer's block. I guess my vanity squelched any hope of creativity. I didn't want to say anything in particular, I just wanted to be heard. I had written the first page or two of several best sellers before giving up. I grew tired of running into walls. A sense of frustration continued to swell inside.

Not long after I had given up, I encountered someone who helped me put things into proper perspective. Psychologist Rollo May came to St. Louis to give a lecture. After his talk Dr. May took questions from the audience. One question came from a young man who asked something about anxiety. After a short pause May answered as much as he could and then finished by saying that there were certain aspects of this issue which still puzzled him. The young man immediately protested, "But you wrote a book about this!" After a longer pause May took a deep breath and said, "A man does not write a book when he knows something. He writes a book when he is struggling with something." As I sat there with mouth wide open my writer's block began to crumble.

Humility has never been a popular topic. We will soon begin exploring the reasons why. Humility is a virtue which, as a culture, we are trying to struggle without. The development of an identity is too often a fight for superiority and a flight from inferiority. We cannot attain happiness, however, until we accept the things about ourselves which we cannot change. Even the "not good" things.

This book does not offer the key to good looks, total happiness or profound wisdom. I begin with the hypothesis that humility is essential for healthy human growth. This work reflects my struggle and my conviction.

A Psychology of Humility

CHAPTER ONE

Why Humility?

The curious paradox is that when I
accept myself as I am, then I change.
— Carl Rogers

Birth is wrapped in humility.[1] We come into this world helpless. Hopefully, at the time and place of our births there are adults who know how to deal with our powerlessness. Without these caretakers we could not survive.

Perhaps the first thing we learn about ourselves during infancy is how impotent we are. As the months pass we gather more and more evidence to support this belief. We learn how helpless young children are and how powerful adults are. Indeed, young children see adulthood as the epitome of power and control.

Our childish image of the all powerful adult can have lasting effects. We try to grow into our own image of what an adult should be. Toward this end we strive for total self-sufficiency, the antithesis of the powerlessness we knew as children.

Fortunately, many people come to realize that complete self-sufficiency is not only unnecessary, it is impossible. We can never be as powerful as the heroes in a child's dreams.

Though this discovery represents a crucial stage in healthy adult development, it occurs in too few people because our culture does not help adults to live with their limitations. We, as a society, like to put our best foot forward. We eat, sleep, breathe and dress for success. We enjoy feeling confident. We find satisfaction in expressing ourselves to others, especially if we are assured of their approval.

If anything threatens these human pleasures, it will certainly be considered undesirable. Enter humility. Because our culture believes humility serves only to help people accept themselves as failures, we avoid it as we do anything associated with failure. This situation led George Salloway to ask, "Could it be that we have misunderstood humility as much as our age has misunderstood us?"[2]

Focusing only on success, triumph, change and self-sufficiency results in an inadequate understanding of ourselves. We do not spend our lives improving all aspects of our being.

Humility helps us live with our flaws, defects and limitations. But these limitations do not make us failures. Rather, they are inherent in our humanity. Humility does not produce failure and yet it recognizes failure as a fact of life.

What happens when we fail? What happens when we do not live up to the image of success? Here may lie the greatest single flaw in western industrial societies. We seem to believe that the only direction is up. Consequently, people have a very difficult time accepting the dimensions of our being which are not constantly improving.

When I began my research on humility my first finding was that this quality may be our most neglected virtue. Textbooks on psychology, psychiatry, human development and education have virtually ignored humility. These scientific approaches to the study of humankind—consistent with the values of our culture—focus on the development of potential. Rarely could I find a discussion on living with life's limitations.

What is interesting about this situation is that, historically, science has done its best to humble us. Copernicus, for example, violated everyone's self-image when he denied that the earth is the center of the universe. Later, Darwin came along and claimed we evolved from animals. Freud then told us that we are driven by virtually uncontrollable forces that dwell deep within us. More recently, B.F. Skinner has told us that we are manipulated by external forces which are, largely, beyond our control.

Science has certainly tried to humble us and yet it has taken no responsibility for the possible consequences. On numerous occasions science has told us that we are not what we would like to be without offering advice on how to live with this. This is an indication of how incomplete is the scientific view of humankind. We cannot get a clear picture of the human condition by relying on science alone.

After I had researched the scientific studies of human values and behavior, I remembered hearing about humility some years before while I was doing research on Alcoholics Anonymous. As I investigated this source I found a goldmine of information.

A.A. is based on a set of principles called the "Twelve Steps." The Twelve Steps are "a group of principles, spiritual in their nature, which, if practiced as a way of life, can expel the obsession to drink and enable the sufferer to become happily and usefully whole."[3] Furthermore, in the words of A.A. co-founder Bill W., "The attainment of greater humility is the foundation principle of each of A.A.'s Twelve Steps."[4]

I had been aware of the effectiveness of A.A. for some time. I believed all along that this organization represented the most potent form of treatment for alcoholism. I was intrigued by their accomplishments. Previously, I had studied A.A. from the perspective of a psychologist and I had missed their meaning. During the course of researching this book, I returned with a wider lens.

A.A. members make it clear that their program is not as much a psychological process as it is a spiritual process. Instead of focusing on themselves, they move their attention to a Higher Power. If we could zero in on a single dimension which distinguishes A.A. from other forms of treatment, it may be this sojourn from the psychological domain to the spiritual realm. The more secular or scientific approaches to treatment do not offer such an awakening.

The attainment of humility is valued so highly in A.A. because only with humility can a person develop his spiritual dimension. Paradoxically, developing one's spirituality leads to a deeper understanding and appreciation of humility.

Psychologist Abraham Maslow proposed a hierarchy of human needs which stated that the satisfaction of our biological needs leads to an awareness of psychological needs. If these psychological needs (i.e. security, a sense of belonging, love, self-esteem) are met, the individual moves on to consider the "higher" or spiritual dimensions of life.

But this widely accepted theory is not as simple as it may appear. Many people have their biological needs met and still never develop an awareness of the world of feelings and interpersonal relationships. Likewise, many people seem to do very well psychologically and yet never develop an understanding or concern for spirituality.

The connection between the biological and the psychological dimensions is beyond the interests of this book. But the linkage between our psychological nature and our spiritual nature relates directly to humility.

Humility is the bridge between our psychological and our spiritual dimensions. Psychologically, we can describe "how" one begins to develop humility. We can also explain how our culture has hindered this process. Indeed I could write many pages on the psychological aspects of humility. But if I remained only in the psychological arena, I could not explain "why" humility is so important to human development.

The first stages in the development of humility are psychological processes. The lion's share of our discussion will focus on this phase of development. Once humility has become a part of one's character, that individual will move toward becoming spiritual. Because humility begins in the psychological realm and moves into the spiritual dimension, we need two levels to our definition of humility.

Psychologically speaking, humility is the acceptance of our imperfection. It does not prohibit self-expression. Nor does it rule out pride in one's accomplishments. Humility in no way limits human potential. Rather humility allows us to accept the limitations of our potential. Psychologically, humility implies the acceptance of ourselves.

Spiritually, humility describes an acceptance of our place in the universe. With humility we open ourselves up to the possibility that God exists. Humility does not point us to God and yet it allows us to receive God. We accept the fact that there is more to the universe than our imperfect eyes can see and we are not threatened by the existence of a more powerful being. Humility allows us to marvel at the majesty of the universe.

We can begin to understand the value of humility through a consideration of human psychology. But we must keep in mind that we are driven to develop our potential. There is a spiritual dimension in all of us waiting to become actualized.

Pragmatic Humility

Humility applies directly to our lives. Consequently the absence of humility also has an immediate effect on our being. Without humility we tend to place severe and unrealistic demands upon ourselves. This in turn leads to emotional overload and stunted growth. Those who admit and accept their foibles are freer from excess emotional turmoil.

Abraham Maslow, in his studies of self-actualized people, described the importance of humility in the life of the psychologically healthy person:

> Healthy individuals find it possible to accept themselves and their own nature without chagrin or complaint. . . . They can accept their own human nature in the stoic style, with all its shortcomings, with all its discrepancies from the ideal image without feeling real concern. It would convey the wrong impression to say that they are self-satisfied. What we must say rather is that they can take the frailties and sins, weaknesses and evils of human nature in the same unquestioning spirit with which one accepts the characteristics of nature.[5]

Emotionally healthy people realize that some things do not change. Certain aspects of our being stay fixed. This adds consistency to our lives. But consistency is small consolation for the pain that can come with limitations such as a permanent physical handicap. We can never do all that we can imagine. We are all handicapped in this regard. In my mind's eye I see myself sitting at a piano playing music for thousands of adoring fans. It feels wonderful. My fantasy turns to frustration, however, when I remember I am tone deaf.

People usually keep these fantasies and frustrations to themselves. Perhaps we all have our own private emotional roller coasters. We all struggle to accept things about ourselves which we do not want to accept. Rarely do we share this encounter with humility.

Not only can we live with our limitations, we can learn from our imperfection. An accurate understanding of ourselves gives us a clearer sense of direction. Our talents and limitations interact to produce a purpose in our lives. Talents are easy to accept. Our flaws, of course, are more difficult to deal with.

Humility can help us find meaning and purpose in life. Bill W. described how humility contributed to his life's mission:

> Absolute humility would consist of a state of complete freedom from myself, freedom from all the claims that my defects of character now lay so heavily upon me. Perfect humility would be a full willingness, in all times and places, to find and to do the will of God.[6]

Bill W. believed that perfect humility could be approached but never achieved. We can move toward it, but never grasp it.

We must move toward an understanding and acceptance of our limitations. Without this we lose a genuine sense of ourselves. An overestimation of self leads to a tremendous amount of identity confusion. Theologian Samuel Dresner described the situation as follows:

> The sin of which modern man is most frequently found guilty is that of "self-sufficiency." It is the belief that man is sufficient unto himself and needs no divine authority and guide. It is the certainty that man is

capable of fathoming all secrets, of controlling all events, of mastering all situations, even of achieving a utopian society of peace and prosperity which would endure until the end of time.[7]

So much of our identity comes from our relationships. How we relate to others and how they relate to us teaches us important things about ourselves. An illusion of self-sufficiency represses the awareness of our need for relationships and consequently we lose our grasp on who we are. We believe we need nothing when we feel we are everything. Humility can replace this myth with a certain wisdom.

Alfred Lord Tennyson called humility "the highest virtue, mother of them all." Confucius described it as "the solid foundation of all the virtues." "The only wisdom we can hope to acquire is the wisdom of humility; humility is endless," wrote T.S. Eliot. We will never be perfect. This is one of the few absolutes we have to guide us in life.

Many great thinkers have praised humility. But why? What is it about humility that can add to the quality of one's life? A.A. describes humility as "a word often misunderstood. To those who have made progress in A.A., it amounts to a clear recognition of what and who we really are, followed by a sincere attempt to become what we could be."[8] Humility provides one with a firm sense of self and a direction in life.

Even though we rarely discuss humility, deep inside isn't there a respect that has survived our neglect? People still value humility in friends. It's nice to know people who are not always comparing themselves with you. Constant interpersonal competition can be exhausting. Keeping up with those crazy Joneses may be the number one cause of stress today.

They say virtue is its own reward, but we can be more

specific than that. Humility allows us to know ourselves as we really are. It allows insight to reach much further than it otherwise could. There are aspects of our being which will grow until we die. In these areas our potential is virtually limitless. Few people have difficulty facing these dimensions.

There are also areas of our being where growth stops. Examples could be physical growth, musical or artistic ability, or intellectual development. To protect an unhealthy self-esteem, people can deny these dimensions access into consciousness. They are seen as unacceptable defects. Sometimes these flaws are even justified as penance for sins committed in past lives, a cross to bear in shame and misery. But if we do not allow our imperfections into consciousness, we do not know who we are. If we do not accept our limitations, we do not accept who we are.

Some people think that humility pertains to an acceptance of an inferior social role. This is not necessarily the case. If a woman is born into a male dominated society, for example, she may decide to accept this position and live her life in the prescribed manner. Her alternative, however, would be to attempt to change the status of women in that society. She has the right to decide. Neither course of action by itself would describe her in terms of humility.

Humility involves accepting the aspects of our world which cannot be improved. Indeed it can be a very difficult task deciding exactly what can be changed and what cannot. The wisdom needed to make this distinction comes only after we allow ourselves the right to imperfection. I will recognize imperfection only if I allow for imperfection. If I do not allow for my own imperfection, I will never really know myself.

We run the risk of making a mistake every time we make a decision. Deciding which aspects of our lives we would like to change but cannot poses a genuine dilemma. We know we are going to die. We know we are dependent on food, water and air. We cannot change our race, who our biological parents are, or our past. We can change our attitudes, however, toward these things. People born without limbs must face the truth that the arm or leg will not eventually develop. And though science and technology have made correctable things which were once considered permanent (e.g. gender, eye color, nose size and wrinkles), human flaws are not on the list of endangered species.

There are no shortcuts to knowing which areas of our lives are unfortunately permanent. We can only learn from an honest appraisal of our experience. Which endeavors have I repeatedly given my best try and yet have come up empty? Which walls am I constantly running into? If we accept the fact that we do not have to be competent at everything, the answers will come.

Once we accept our imperfection there is a world full of people we can relate to. We can enjoy discussing things we are proud of and struggle and laugh together about our disappointments. Accepting a humble attitude toward life means resigning from the constant competition to be the best. If happiness belonged only to the "best" person in the world, then there would only be one happy person; and that person would probably be very lonely.

Humility does not mean living a life completely void of competition. And above all it does not mean abandoning feelings of pride. Humility, rather, is one part of being which, to an extent, pervades our entire being. It serves as a constant reminder that we are not, nor do we have to be, perfect or completely self-sufficient.

I consider humility a virtue for three reasons. First, it promotes growth within the individual. It aids in the acceptance and development of self. This presents a paradox. We grow when we accept the fact that certain dimensions of ourselves will develop no more. Psychologist Carl Rogers wrote ". . . when I accept myself as I am, I change."⁹

Secondly, besides helping us with the acceptance of self, our interpersonal relationships deepen when imperfection becomes acceptable. We can relate to others with more honesty and self-expression when we are able to share what might be called the darker side of ourselves. The cold plastic facade can be replaced with warm human feelings. We will discuss this in greater detail in the next chapter.

The third reason I consider humility a virtue relates to how it is attained. Humility, wisdom, courage, curiosity, hope, love, patience and all other virtues come only as they are earned. Even the most spoiled child will never receive virtue as a gift. Perhaps this is why spoiled children are so angry.

It may be said that human growth is the process of adding virtues to one's character. The feeling of encountering a new virtue seems to be a very rewarding yet highly personal experience. Take, for instance, the jubilation Ebenezer Scrooge felt after he acquired kindness. Or the ecstasy Oliver Twist experienced when he finally found love. In Oz, the Cowardly Lion, the Scarecrow and the Tin Man all represent the struggle and triumph involved in achieving different virtues. The lesson is simple; you work for your virtues.

The *Wizard of Oz* deserves a bit more attention here. The story focuses on the plight of five main characters. Dorothy searches for a home, the Cowardly Lion for courage, the Scarecrow for wisdom, the Tin Man for love and the Witch for revenge. Fortunately, everyone but the wicked Witch completes their task. But there is someone else in the story who manages to develop a virtue. Someone who has never received much attention, in spite of the fact that without him there would be no story. The lesson we can learn from this character is as valuable as any lesson in the story.

The Wizard of Oz learns humility. His "wizardry" is one of the greatest literary descriptions of a facade of greatness. This trembling soul hides behind the mask, regalia and legend of the mighty sage and monarch of Oz. He lives strictly on reputation. Behind his disguise he uses his "might" to protect his impotence.

Once the wizard is caught, his life changes drastically for the better. He takes what little courage he has and invests it in honesty. He admits to himself and to Oz that he is a fraud. He then presents himself as someone who cannot just hand out virtues. But as a simple and, now, honest man he can clearly see the virtue already present in others. The Wizard becomes humble enough to admire his fellow beings. The story ends with the Wizard happily rubbing elbows with people he once considered inferior. The mean, lonely Wizard not-so-magically changes into a happy, humble person.

Just as the Lion, Scarecrow and Tin Man originally sought virtue in the form of something tangible, so too do people in our real world. Often we encounter individuals who base their self-worth on what they have rather than what they are. Psychoanalyst Erich Fromm called this the "to have or to be" dilemma.

To Have Or To Be

There are dimensions of our being which cannot be taken away by others. These dimensions comprise who we are. There are also things very important in our lives which can be supplied or removed by circumstances beyond our control. These entities represent what we have. Who we are and what we have are as different as inside and outside. Yet the two are often confused.

Identities based on possessions are very dangerous. "If I am what I have and if what I have is lost, who then am I?"[10] One way to reduce the risk is to spend your life guarding what you have. We call this life style paranoia. It doesn't amount to much of a life, but it is one way to pass the years.

Some people see advantages in basing one's self-esteem on the accumulation of goods. If I believe I am no one of consequence and I see new clothes, a new car and a home computer as a means of becoming someone significant, I'll buy it all. And for a while this can work. Unfortunately, like all addictions, this story ends tragically. (Unless, of course, I die before I collect enough possessions to convince me this is not working.)

A secure identity begins in a secure environment. Family and friends need to provide a dependable and somewhat predictable environment for the growing child. As the child grows into adulthood, the security of the environment becomes incorporated into the inner self. At this point, though the adult still needs other people, there exists a feeling of security which cannot be manipulated by others. This security can be described as the feeling "I am somebody with a unique set of talents and limitations. And I can live with this."

When we believe that we really are respectable beings with meaning in our lives, then all the material goods become even more enjoyable. We can see that they are toys rather than indispensable parts of our being. The home computer can teach us new things. The car can take us places we might not otherwise go. Both are helpful, yet hardly necessary.

To feel secure in one's being establishes a tremendously strong foundation to grow upon. If I respect myself, I re-

spect my inclinations. Curiosity can rocket to the corners of
the universe. And if I respect myself I will not be ashamed of
my faults. Nor will I forget that I have faults. G.K.
Chesterton summed it up accurately when he said, "It is
always the secure who are humble."

Pride

> How in the world did a nice emotion like pride get
> elected first of the seven deadly sins? Why is not pride
> one of the cardinal virtues? Self-respect, self-esteem,
> and self-confidence—all ingredients of pride are essen-
> tial elements to adaptation.   — *Willard Gaylin*

While humility has been neglected, pride has been
routinely maligned. *Webster's New International Dictionary* defines pride as "inordinate self-esteem; an unrealistic conceit
or superiority in talents, beauty, wealth, rank, etc." *The
Random House Dictionary* defines the term as "a high or
inordinate opinion of one's own dignity, importance, merit,
or superiority, whether as cherished in the mind or as dis-
played in bearing, conduct, etc."

Is pride really so bad? *The American Heritage Dictionary*
describes pride as "a sense of one's own proper dignity and
value; self-respect." This represents a much more
sympathetic view of the concept, a view which has other
supporters including Willard Gaylin.

> As a psychoanalyst in mid-twentieth-century America,
> I view pride as a virtue and its absence the deficiency of
> our time. The restoration of pride is a major goal in
> treatment. Self-respect and self-value are essential
> components of the capacity for pleasure and perform-
> ance which underlie the healthy (good) life.[11]

The controversy within the mental health profession mirrors the contradictions revealed when we compared dictionaries. Psychiatrist Harry Stack Sullivan saw pride as "an elaborate self-deception, a facade, a strategem that excludes from awareness some inadequacy in the self."[12] Obviously, Sullivan did not see pride as desirable a characteristic as Gaylin does.

The consequences of such a controversy, or should I say confusing mess, are potentially severe. Counselors and therapists treat people with emotional and psychological problems. Many patients suffer from an inability to "get in touch with their feelings." But getting in touch with one's feelings becomes much more difficult when "authorities" completely disagree on which labels match which feelings. This makes it very difficult for people to communicate feelings. The confusion created by the mental health experts serves to increase the demands for their services. What is even worse is that this confusion decreases the likelihood that treatment will be successful.

So who is right? Is pride healthy or unhealthy? The answer is that pride is a very positive characteristic which can easily become destructive. When feelings of pride turn destructive, however, they are properly called feelings of conceit, arrogance or superiority. Pride describes a feeling of positive regard for ourselves, a very healthy feeling.

In the beginning of this section I wrote that whereas humility has been neglected, pride has been maligned. Without humility, pride becomes conceit and arrogance. Because we as a culture have virtually ignored the virtue humility, the value we place on pride is understandably low.

The proud yet humble man feels good about himself for who he is. He does not need to elevate himself on the failures of others. Because he is also aware of his limitations, he retains a feeling of admiration for humanity. His humility allows him to have pride in others. This is the feeling, "I'm damn good at such and such, but all and all I know I'm no *better* than anyone else."

Humility keeps pride from turning into feelings of superiority. Feelings of superiority create a distance between the individual and the people in his world. Without humility, pride decays into superiority, arrogance and conceit. In this case, "I'm good" turns into "I'm better than all the losers."

Yet humility owes a debt of gratitude to pride as well. Without feelings of pride, we run the risk of being excessively passive. We would be more likely to fall prey to complacency. Feeling proud is the emotional reward for doing our best. It serves as a tremendous motivator to actualize our potential.

Humility and pride compose a dialectic; each concept gives the other meaning. Without humility, pride becomes arrogance and conceit. Without pride, humility becomes passivity and complacency. Together, pride and humility form a foundation for healthy growth. If we begin to pay more attention to humility, pride may one day become a virtue.

Abraham Maslow recognized the need for pride in the development of mental health. He believed that all people in our society (with a few pathological exceptions) have a need for a stable, firmly based, usually high evaluation of themselves, for self-respect, and for the esteem of others.[13] We like to feel good about ourselves. We want others to like us. Furthermore, we like to think that this state of affairs will continue.

After an extensive review of anthropological research, Maslow concluded, ". . . all peoples reported in the literature seemed to have pride, to prefer to be liked, to seek respect and status, to avoid anxiety."[14] So what is there to be ashamed of? When we feel free to talk about pride, we find that just about everyone pursues this feeling. Why should people *not* want to feel good about themselves?

Pride does not separate us from other people as superiority does. Feeling proud makes us feel truly alive and good about the world. The feeling is never a problem; how it is communicated to others can be. Most people admire pride in a friend as long as they can also see a sense of humility. It's a great experience to have friends who, no matter how good they feel about themselves, can talk with you eye to eye, heart to heart. Friends who do not allow their success to lift them above you.

Mature pride, however, will not make you popular with everyone. In our world we have an ample supply of bitter people. Bitter people don't like people who feel good about themselves. Bitter people usually vascillate between intense feelings of inferiority and equally strong feelings of superiority. They spend their lives living above and beneath others. It's a lonely life. Their superiority represents a feeble defense constructed in an attempt to maintain fleeting feelings of dignity. Bitter people also have a very difficult time asking for help. This would crack their mighty facade. It would be above and beyond the intentions of this book to discuss in depth how to cure bitterness. Hopefully it will suffice to say that no one has, as yet, found a panacea. But I will propose a method for stemming the tide of bitterness.

We can allow ourselves the right to our own feelings. If someone disapproves of my proud feelings, I can still keep them. My pride won't hurt anyone else and it makes my life happier. My pride does not make me feel superior to anyone else. I can still talk with friends eye to eye and heart to heart. Pride does not cut me off from other people. In fact, it gives me a greater appreciation of the world I live in.

If we do not feel good about ourselves, it may not be

possible to feel good about others. As people, we have so many things in common. Though not always consciously, we all have an opinion on the value of human beings. Before we meet someone, we already have a certain mind set which carries the answer to the question, "How much respect does this person deserve based solely on the fact that he is a human being?" In other words, how much value is inherent in humanity? If we find little value in our own being, how positive can our answer be?

Am I proud to be a person? Does knowing that I am a living breathing human being give me a sense of satisfaction? Do I take pride in people? If we can answer these questions in the affirmative, our self-esteem will never drop into the dangerous zone. If there is some value inherent in human nature, then we will see some value in everyone, including ourselves. If we believe that we all share the right to a healthy level of respect and dignity we will never develop pervasive feelings of inferiority or superiority.

Before We Go On

There is a plethora of controversy within the disciplines that study the human condition. People are so complex that we, at this point in time, have only two principles which everyone seems to accept.

First, people age toward death and there are physical, psychological and emotional consequences to the aging process. Exactly what these consequences are remains unsettled. There does seem to be a consensus, however, that the effects of aging reach deep into our being.

The second principle which has escaped controversy is that people need people. Birth involves two parents and a child. After the child enters the world, he cannot survive by himself. Beside physical dependence, the developing person needs others in order to develop a secure identity and a sense of well-being. Neglected children withdraw into themselves. Such children rarely acquire the ability to reach out and ask for help. They usually suffer in silence.

In our attempt to understand humility, these two points are extremely important. Both the aging process and our need for other people are humbling experiences. They remind us of what we have to work with in life.

If we do not understand our limitations, we do not understand our being. If we cannot accept our limitations, we cannot accept our being. Humility is a necessary virtue if we are to accept and to be honest with ourselves. It does not restrict us to a stoic acceptance of tragedy. Humility is quite compatible with feelings of pride, joy and self-respect.

CHAPTER TWO

People Who Need People

It is always the secure who are humble.
— G.K. Chesterton

Humans have formed societies ever since our species came to life. There are many reasons why people throughout time have lived in tribes, clans, villages and kingdoms. The most important need fulfilled by social groupings is the need for protection. There is strength in numbers. This strength is crucial in defending against disease, wild animals, foreign invaders and starvation. Our social skills are very important survival skills.

Historical and anthropological research consistently attests that people need people. If early man had not been able to form cooperative tribes and villages, we never would have gotten past the caveman stage. In order for people to live and work together, we must admit (at least to ourselves) that we need each other. Our motivation for living a life of cooperation comes from the realization that we, as individuals, are not completely self-sufficient.

Today we are just as far from self-sufficiency as at any point in history. We depend on physicians, automobiles, dentists, televisions, teachers, microwave ovens, babysitters, refrigerators, therapists, lawyers, drugs and money—to name only a few things. At no other time in history have people had so many things that we just could not do without.

If the aim of modern technology is to create self-sufficiency, then its aim is to put itself out of business. This doesn't seem likely. But as long as there are consumers arrogant enough to believe that a certain product will free them from needing others, that product will be bought and cherished. And before too long there will be another product advertised with the same promise.

Healthy people do not feel defeated when they realize their need for other people. Indeed it can be comforting to know that other people need us. Relationships take on a much deeper meaning when people realize we need each other. Today we desperately need each other. I hope our society develops the humility to admit it.

In order to develop this humility, however, our society will have to change. Samuel Dresner wrote, ". . . our society does not hold the humble man in high esteem. Certainly society does not often set him up as an ideal to imitate."[1] Instead we idealize the person who is an obvious success, the individual who seems to have done it all by himself.

The most popular means of demonstrating self-sufficiency is through competition. People who try to deny their need for others are constantly in competition. Defeating someone else can be a way of communicating, "I don't need you because I'm better than you." Bitter people live this way. They live a never ending struggle to prove they are O.K. all by themselves. Their victories are temporary and unsatisfying and their defeats are reminders of how painful relationships are. Such people cannot maintain good feelings about themselves nor can they resign from the competition.

It would be a mistake to claim that all competition reflects an absence of social skills. This is clearly not the case.

When we are grounded in healthy human relationships, competition can enrich our lives. Competition can help foster feelings of pride. Educators know that competition used correctly can motivate a student to fulfill potential.

The difference between the healthy and the unhealthy person is that the healthy person can, by his own volition, step out of the competitive arena. The healthy person can return to a sincere cooperative life style. The unhealthy individual remains in the ring, alternating between superiority and inferiority until exhaustion sets in. Then there is only inferiority.

Inferiority

The person with pervasive feelings of inferiority leads a tragic life. The only rewards he knows are intermittent feelings of superiority which really only serve as opportunities to release anger at others. This person rarely, if ever, experiences happiness and his hopes for the future are usually exaggerated fantasies.

Due to a dismal self-esteem, this soul cannot realistically see himself as building a satisfactory life, nor can he envision life without the constant competition. Humility is not in this man's vocabulary because he sees himself as having too many attributes which are completely unacceptable.

Feelings of inferiority almost completely inhibit self-expression. People who feel inferior have the attitude, "If people really knew me, they'd know just how terrible I really am." So they construct facades in an attempt to keep others from seeing how horrible they are. Life behind the facade is very lonely. No one gets to know such people as they really are. Their true self remains hidden and alone.

People who feel inferior may be ashamed of many areas of their being. They feel that these dimensions are so much

worse than what other people live with. If people with
inferiority feelings are encouraged to share their feelings
with others, they often find that many of the things they
were ashamed of are things they have in common with
everyone else. The secrecy and withdrawal which are in-
tended to protect this individual, actually increase their
misery.

People with feelings of inferiority are excellent candi-
dates for group counseling. Though it often takes quite a bit
of encouragement to take such a risk, the rewards can be
tremendous. When I was just out of graduate school, I
began working in a counseling center in suburban St. Louis.
One of my duties was to conduct a counseling group for
adults between the ages of 25 and 40. Most of my training
was in individual and family therapy, and I felt a bit unsure
of my skills as a group counselor. There were seven adults in
the group, most of whom agreed that their problem was that
they were "too sensitive." They all had fairly successful
careers. They were basically lonely people whose therapists
recommended group counseling because they were not
finding satisfaction in interpersonal relationships.

The group got off to a very rocky start—seven people
who were afraid of any self-expression, each waiting for the
others to go first. By the end of four sessions, the clients had
not changed, but I had developed more intense feelings of
inadequacy. I didn't know how to get these people to open
up. I had tried everything in the books. I didn't even understand why they all kept returning to the weekly sessions.
Looking back, I guess they all sensed that they had so much
in common.

Finally, in the fifth session, one of the group members
taught me what I needed to know (and I will be forever
grateful). I had the feeling that they all had plenty to say—
more like bursting at the seams—and yet wouldn't let it out.

Out of my own exasperation and in a desperate voice, I confronted a young woman in the group, "Ya know, Maureen, I get the feeling you've got a lot to say for yourself but for some reason you think you can't. Now I know you can't tell me what it is, but can you tell me why you can't tell us about yourself?" After a short pause she replied, "Because I feel so inferior to everyone." I then asked the group, "Does anyone else feel this way?" Slowly six other hands were raised.

At that point the group came alive. For the next couple of sessions we talked *about* inferiority—what it is, why it happens, and what can be done about it. The solutions we discussed were not nearly as therapeutic as the fact that they were all sharing things about themselves which they had previously kept hidden. Eventually they moved from an objective (or classroom-like) discussion of inferiority to a much more personal talk about the feelings of inferiority in their lives. They gradually lost their inferiority about their feelings of inferiority. As time passed, feelings of inferiority began to wane.

This group was successful because these "inferior" people had so much talent. My role in their treatment was more or less incidental. They had all the tools to help each other and they were eventually able to risk compassion. I learned so much from these people and this experience. There is so much potential being strangled by feelings of inferiority.

There is a final point of interest concerning this group. Because they grew close to each other, we did not run into the problem of newborn feelings of superiority. (Although several people went through stages of anger). They grew to like each other too much to distance themselves from each other. They felt no need to place the others beneath them.

People with painful inferiority feelings rarely treat

themselves. If they remain isolated, not asking for help, their prognosis is poor. Left alone, the occasional feeling of superiority begins to disappear. The individual may develop a sense of hopelessness and helplessness. This state of being is described psychologically as depression.

It is not easy for people with low self-esteem to ask for help. Asking for help means admitting the need for help. The facade then weakens and the individual becomes even more vulnerable.

One reason low self-esteem people find it so difficult to ask for help relates to a defense mechanism called projection. When self-esteem drops to a certain point it becomes intolerable. At this stage the psyche must find a way to handle it. One way is to "project" these feelings on to other people. The low self-esteem person then forgets how bad he feels about himself and instead concentrates on what others think about him. Since he unconsciously feels bad about himself, he now believes that the people in his world think he is more or less worthless. This individual interprets his situation as, "I don't feel bad about myself but nobody else seems to like me."

If I feel that other people don't like me, I probably won't ask them for help. How could I trust them? The cycle grows vicious. Low self-esteem ◗ isolation ◗ lower self-esteem ◗ greater isolation ◗ on and on. The cycle can be broken by increasing self-esteem and reducing the individual's isolation. Honest, caring relationships make for the most effective form of treatment.

Another unhealthy way to handle inferiority is through prejudice and bigotry. The bigot will write off large groups of people as inferior. He feels that by virtue of his race, sex, nationality, health or whatever, he is better than they are. This keeps him from falling to the bottom of the pile. The bigot can also blame this for his own problems like taxes, crime, unemployment, inflation, etc.

The bigot, however, lives with intense feelings of inferiority. The more intense his prejudice, the more intense are his feelings of inferiority. His prejudice allows him intermittent feelings of superiority. These feelings empower him to vent his anger at the world. There is no such thing as an emotionally healthy bigot.

Prejudice and bigotry are attitudes we could all do without and yet so many of us have these feelings. In our struggle to feel good about ourselves we are often tempted to believe that, even at our worst, we are better than a particular group of people. Renowned sociologist Erving Goffman noted our tendency toward prejudice:

> In an important sense there is only one complete unblushing male in America: a young, married, white, urban, northern heterosexual Protestant father of college education, fully employed, of good complexion, weight and height, and a recent record in sports.[2]

According to Goffman only a person such as this has a chance of being immune from instant social disqualification. All the rest of us can expect to serve as someone's cause for disgust. But we must keep in mind that where there is prejudice, there are feelings of inferiority.

So how does inferiority develop? Feelings of inferiority develop on the basis of how we interpret our life experiences. Experiences which convince us that we are not as good as, and consequently do not belong with, others are called humiliations. The epitome of humiliation is the experience of being laughed at. In such an experience someone controls you, causes you pain, and then delights in your misery. Ethnic jokes are a common form of humiliation. More severe forms of humiliation include the process of tar and feathering undesirables. In colonial America, petty criminals were chained to stocks in the town square where passersby would hurl garbage and insults. Today we consider such a humiliation to be a cruel and unusual form of punishment. Furthermore, we cannot rehabilitate someone by humiliating them. Humiliation leads to feelings of inferiority which, in turn, often leads to more anti-social behavior.

The humiliated feel ostracized from the community. They feel alone, unprotected and vulnerable. It is difficult for one person to humiliate another. Humiliated individuals feel that their oppressor represents a larger group of people. The rape victim, for instance, often feels humiliated by the attack. She may feel dirty, violated and helpless. She may think that people are blaming her for what happened. Maybe her family and friends cannot give her sufficient support during this crisis. Perhaps she will not even report the crime because she fears the possible reactions of others.

In court, the degradation may continue with the defense counsel accusing her of either lying or encouraging the attack. In other words, the victim frequently feels misunderstood and unacceptable to others, even loved ones. She feels humiliated not only by the rapist but by her family, friends and society.

When people are humiliated beyond a tolerable point they become withdrawn, angry and afraid. They lose the ability to forgive. Once they are too defeated to fight back in reality, they begin to fight back in fantasy. In the mind's eye, they replay the humiliations over and over. Often they will create a new ending where the oppressor receives his just deserts. During this phase the individual may, given the opportunity, work up the motivation to assert himself in an attempt to overcome his humiliation. The little boy who is picked on and afraid to fight back may gradually work up the nerve to defend himself. If no action is forthcoming, however, the fantasies will eventually cease and the individual will be forced to live with the fear of future humiliations. He feels helpless and sees no way out.

People who feel inferior place themselves in a suffocating bind. These people live in a state of uncertainty. They are not sure what other people like, how other people feel, or how they should act. Consequently, they cling to any type of certainty they can find. The thing they are most certain about, however, is their inferiority. It is the one thing they feel has been absolutely proven by experience. And if they are ever in doubt, they can always go out and once again prove their worthlessness. Their low self-esteem is painful, but it is predictable. If they change their opinion of themselves, they may be faced with (at least temporarily) total uncertainty. Mental health professionals call this the crisis of change.

We now come to a most confusing point. I must make it clear that humiliation has nothing to do with humility. The similarity between these two words is most unfortunate. Our disgust for the experience of humiliation biases us in our evaluation of humility. But there is no connection between the two.

A humiliating experience leads to feelings of inferiority. Being taunted by a crowd, booed off the field, or given the dunce cap are all examples of humiliation. Inferiority results from repeated humiliations. Humility, on the other hand, results from the acceptance of our imperfection. We do not learn this acceptance by way of humiliation. We encounter our limitations and learn to accept them through humbling experiences.

Humbling experiences remind us that human beings are

faced with limitations. The fact that I have limitations gives me something in common with everyone else. There are some restrictions we all share and others which vary among individuals. In neither case do my restrictions make me less than human. On the contrary, they prove my humanity.

The death of a loved one can be a very humbling experience. Because we are mortals we must live with the ways of life. In working through grief, we need to come to terms with our humanity. Can I accept the fact that my loved one is gone? That I can't bring her back? That someday I too will die?

The passage of time presents another humbling experience. A thirty year-old graduate student named Gary once told me, "Last week I was driving home at the usual time— about 5:30. I saw the sun going down . . . I stared at it for a while and then started getting really upset. I began to cry and thought, 'This is it. I'm losing my mind.' " He was now fighting back the tears.

Gary felt his life was slipping away. After college he had "taken off for a few years." He thought that when the time came he could just start a career and live the middle class life. When he eventually returned to graduate school to study business, he did poorly. He learned that he was not happy with a career in business, but he lacked the enthusiasm for any alternative. He became overwhelmed when he realized that the clock was running but he was going nowhere.

For Gary the sunset was symbolic of the passage of time. What made this incident even more traumatic was the fact that Gary had little experience with humility. Previously he thought he could do anything. He felt time would always be on his side because he was special. He did not realize that we all face the same sunset everyday. He also did not know that most of us, at some point in our lives, have similar awakenings.

Gary's experience with the sunset was ultimately a humbling experience. At first, however, it threatened to be a humiliation. He originally thought that only a very weak person would cry over a sunset. He was embarrassed to tell me about it. Once he began to accept such limitations as the passage of time, he developed a more mature outlook on his life. He came to realize that his future would not take shape by magic. Like everyone else, he had to work and worry.

A humbling experience can be painful. When we reconsider our experiences, we sometimes find that what we thought were humiliations may, in fact, be humbling experiences. A humbling experience eventually gives us a greater acceptance of ourselves and a stronger sense of community.

No one should be humiliated by a sunset.

Superiority

In the vast majority of cases, feelings of superiority are attempts to compensate for feelings of inferiority. Both describe how you are different from other people, whether you are better or worse. Once people feel ostracized from a social group, they must come to grips with the feeling of being "not good enough." Since they are unable to join the group, their only alternative is to be "better" than the rest.

People fighting for a position of superiority generally do so by one of three tactics. They either generalize, boot-lick or humiliate.

The technique of generalization involves mastering one specific skill and generalizing the results. These people try to base their self-esteem on their competence in one particular area. If I, for instance, am the best shower nozzle salesman in the state, I may conclude that I can be the best at anything. People who use this strategy to bolster their egos usually have an intense yet very narrow specialty. They will spend countless hours lining up dominoes, polishing pennies, collecting toothpicks or guessing hat sizes. To be the best at tying shoelaces makes them "the best." Generalizers owe a great debt of gratitude to *Guinness' Book of World Records*. Guinness gives them the notoriety and the confirmation that they are indeed the best.

The generalization technique is available to anyone who can find or invent something which they can dominate. Since there are so many possible areas, generalization continues to become a more and more popular approach to attaining feelings of superiority.

A second common approach through which low self-esteem individuals exert superiority is called boot-licking. Boot-lickers are also called sycophants, brown-nosers and yes-men. In this case the low self-esteem person's behavior is guided by a single principle—get close to a powerful person. Morals, ethics and values all go out the window in the pursuit. Loyalty completely disappears and expediency reigns supreme. All is fair in this game.

The only thing that gets in the way of effective boot-licking is conscience. Serious boot-lickers must be willing to prostitute themselves totally. For people with little self-respect, this is not a particularly difficult thing to do. Their low self-esteem can actually help them move into powerful positions. Regardless of appearances, however, because they think so little of themselves, they are miserable. Their conquest of power may bring envy but never happiness.

A third way to compensate for feelings of inferiority is by humiliating others. The rapist, the sadist, the bigot and the child abuser are all examples of low self-esteem people who receive satisfaction by humiliating others. The humiliator thinks that he can lift his status by forcing someone to become more inferior. Unfortunately the humiliator often succeeds. The humiliated individual frequently develops intense feelings of inferiority. The Talmud, in fact, states that humiliating someone in the presence of others is as heinous a crime as murder.

All three forms of superiority have awful consequences. The generalizer must narrow his existence to a very small niche. The boot-licker survives only by abandoning all sense of value and self-respect. The humiliator lives with cruelty and hatred toward all living beings. These strategies compose the most pathological forms of compensation for feelings of inferiority. Their popularity is frightening. The wasted potential and misery caused by these life styles is staggering.

We must keep in mind that any life style which only pursues superiority will isolate the individual. Feelings of superiority distance the individual from the community. It's lonely at the top when you believe there is a real impasse between you and everyone else.

Because of the separation involved, most people do not seek superiority. In fact many will actively avoid it. Certain psychologists have identified a personality trait called "fear of success." Someone is thought to fear success if he consistently sabotages his chances for advancement. One reason people sabotage their success is the fear that success will adversely affect their interpersonal relationships. Often this is an unconscious concern. As children we learned from King Midas that superpower can make us very lonely. These fairy tales have a way of sticking in the back of our minds.

Feelings of superiority become necessary to those who feel inferior and cannot see themselves as being accepted by the rest of humanity. But if I hold on to the belief—"I'm better than everyone else"—I will remain forever alone.

The Illusion of Invulnerability

We are imperfect people living in an imperfect world. We often find it hard to live with this situation. Fortunately, most people do not think of their imperfection as an indication of personal inferiority. Part of the reason for this is that many people refuse to acknowledge their imperfection. It's one thing to accept one's limitations and another to ignore them.

The Greeks had a name for feelings of invincibility—"hubris." Hubris can be described as the refusal to accept one's destiny. The Greeks believed it was a sin because by exaggerating the powers of man, man tried to usurp the powers of the gods. Today hubris describes the feeling of freedom from needs and limitations. It is the denial of how much one is always dependent upon one's fellow man and woman and one's society.[3] Hubris may be thought of as the sin of superiority. It describes a person who feels superior not only to other people but to fate, destiny, God, the gods, nature or any other supreme or sacred force.

How much hubris is there in each of us? Despite the fact that tragedy and misfortune surround us, most of us live day-to-day feeling immune to catastrophe. People keep smoking in spite of overwhelming evidence of its harmful effects. We take chances walking alone at night in places where we probably shouldn't. Why?

Psychologists say these grandiose feelings of security are based on the "illusion of invulnerability." People have a tendency to believe that cancer, car accidents, violent crimes, etc. "won't happen to me." We feel that others are more likely to become victims. We tend to see ourselves as special and less likely to be victimized.[4] This illusion helps keep anxiety to a minimum. With a little denial, the world can become a friendlier place.

There is, however, a dark side to all this. The illusion of invulnerability can, in reality, make us more likely to become victims. When we take chances because we feel protected, we place ourselves in jeopardy. No matter how they feel, smokers run the risk of damaging their bodies. The illusion will not protect us when someone comes to steal our unlocked cars. In short, the popular illusion of invulnerability can make us careless and consequently increase our vulnerability.

Additionally, the illusion of invulnerability makes adjustments to victimization particularly difficult. We maintain the illusion because it is comforting. If reality hits, we lose a tremendous amount of security. A tumor, a mugging or a car accident can threaten our lives and our life styles. We'd prefer to believe that we are always automatically safe. Being forced to recognize our vulnerability to tragedy can produce a crisis. The illusion does not usually return. The crisis of victimization is a time of coming to grips with humility. A certain amount of vulnerability is an inherent part of life. Successful adjustment requires that humility replace illusion.

Healthy Relationships

I've heard it said that the value of a relationship comes through self-expression. I agree. The more self-expression exists between two people, the more they will grow. But this sounds so much easier than it really is. Many people have a knack for talking about themselves and this doesn't seem to help their relationships while other, less vocal people do very well.

Genuine self-disclosure does not mean constantly talking about yourself or taking your clothes off and showing the scar where the horse bit. Self-disclosure means being yourself. Being yourself involves spontaneously sharing what you have to offer the world. You are being yourself when you are not trying to be someone else.

Co-workers and acquaintances see us in particular social roles. They see us as parent, teacher, clerk, policeman, boss, employee or candidate. When we relate to people while performing these duties, our behavior may not be spontaneous. A second grade teacher, for example, may not be inclined to tell her favorite dirty joke at the P.T.A. meeting. It wouldn't be appropriate in her role as teacher. There are some aspects of her being she must wait to share with her close friends.

Some people, unfortunately, take their social roles to bed with them. The behavior appropriate to their position is the only behavior they allow. These people have few friends, but a lot of co-workers and acquaintances.

Though people can be in awe of certain social positions such as doctor, lawyer or Indian chief, we cannot grow to love someone who only knows how to follow protocol. We know someone to the extent that we understand their uniqueness—how this particular Indian chief is different from all the rest.

When I display my individuality, however, I take a risk. I take the chance that who I am is not good enough. If I am not sure if I am good enough, I will leave the decision to others. I will let them decide how I should feel about myself. With young children, this situation is normal. Adults need more self-acceptance.

By the end of adolescence, there should be a secure acceptance of self. The healthy young adult feels he can contribute to a relationship. In spite of this confidence, he has the humility to 1) admit and accept that he has faults and 2) admit that he needs other people to help make the most of his life.

If we accept ourselves in spite of our faults, we have a much easier time sharing our lives. We no longer need to pretend. Our identities are not shrouded in shame. Instead we can learn to delight in who we are. When we accept our flaws, we experience a tremendous feeling of relief. This relief often expresses itself in humor. The ability to laugh at ourselves can be a very reliable coping mechanism. It is an endearing trait which exists in all healthy personalities. In the words of Bill W., "As I get down to my right size and stature, my self-concern and importance become amusing."[5]

Humor is certainly one of humility's rewards. When we allow ourselves to express our embarrassments we usually find it immensely enjoyable. Why do we laugh at Rodney Dangerfield? Because we can all identify with the feeling of being inadequate at times. Comic strip characters Ziggy, Charlie Brown and Herman all entertain us by letting us know we are not alone. Now and then we all feel that life has it in for us.

Have you ever noticed how much easier it is to get along with people who can laugh at themselves? Although there are those who use this as a facade, when it is genuine, it greatly enriches relationships. Humor directed at ourselves communicates humility. This attitude says, "I don't demand that people be perfect." Competitiveness disappears and self-expression usually happens.

Humor can also reverse a humiliation We can't be laughed at by others if we are laughing along with them. Aesop's fable "The Bald Cavalier" tells of a gentleman who loses his wig with a gust of wind. As the crowd laughs, so too does the cavalier. The shared laughter serves to bring all parties closer. The hero's humility and humor save him from humiliation.

When we accept ourselves as we are, we bring a more

enjoyable self into relationships. If we can remember that it's all right to be imperfect there will be more humor in our lives and less jealousy, more individuality and less conformity, more self-expression and less shame.

Conclusion

Humility allows us to accept our need for other people. This is the foundation of healthy relationships. Humility also permits us to love and accept humanity with all its limitations. We don't need to be perfect to be happy. We need humility to be ourselves. Without humility we continuously try to be someone else.

CHAPTER THREE

Children

*It's hard to be humble when you believe
in magic.*
— Rob Furey

I recently came across a series of children's books about values. Each of the 29 books describes a different value and demonstrates that value in the life of a famous person. Helen Keller personifies determination. Johnny Appleseed represents love. Jackie Robinson exemplifies courage. Children incorporate these values into their lives by identifying with heroes. In this set of books the heroes come from the pages of history. Because most children love to collect heroes, I think this approach can be very effective.

The 29 values represented in this series do not include humility. There are several possible reasons for this. First, it could be a simple oversight. Maybe the authors just forgot. Second, the omission could reflect our culture's nonchalance concerning humility as a character trait. Perhaps there would be no demand for a book on humility. Third, maybe the publishers could not find a famous person who truly exemplifies humility. Fourth, perhaps children do not need humility. I vote for reason number four.

Children do not have room in their lives for humility. They have too much going on to concern themselves with the limitations of their being. Children grow like magic. Indeed there is no greater example of magic or miracle in the universe. Childhood is a time for magic, a time for believing that maybe someday I will be able to fly or lift the world or become invisible. Curiosity and imagination are most irrepressible during the early years. The child's limitations may control today but maybe not tomorrow—anything and everything can change.

What should a child accept about himself if most of his physical, psychological and emotional characteristics are only temporary? With technology rapidly changing the way we live, how many expectations are unrealistic for a child? Children have every right to believe in magic.

It's hard to be humble when you believe in magic. Consequently only a very small percentage of children incorporate humility into their personalities. Most things about themselves which are unacceptable can be wished away to when everyone "lives happily ever after." Some children, however, are faced with painful realities which they cannot fantasize away. The abused or neglected child, for example, eventually gives up hope of being lovable. But not even humility can help a child accept himself as unlovable. The magic dies too soon; hopelessness ensues.

Humility is not a part of childhood because the child believes in magic. This does not mean that children do not own feelings of inferiority—most do. Inferiority comes with being subordinate to the rule makers. Parents, teachers and coaches all remind the child of the power he doesn't have. They are also living reminders that someday he will have that power. Inferiority is thought to be temporary; it even serves as incentive for growth.

In psychological terms, magical thinking is a form of denial. Children use this mental mechanism to help tame their world. The child cannot control an overwhelming reality, but he can make modifications in how he perceives reality. Magic can help him deny the permanence of life's difficulties. But the child's magic is only so powerful. If a child becomes too discouraged, he gives up on magic and withdraws into reality (e.g. the abused or neglected child). He may then run away, become depressed, take drugs or commit suicide.

In a healthy environment, the child comes to feel good about many aspects of himself. Children seek opportunities to feel proud. Kids feel wonderful if they can spit the farthest, burp the loudest or bathe the least. They enjoy being able to do things other kids can't. This is how their individuality emerges.

Some children, however, are punished for their individuality. When the important people in a child's world tell him he is worthless, he is in a defenseless position. The child does not yet have the independent character to retain his self-respect in the midst of constant ridicule. A child believes what is told about himself. Before he can accept himself, he needs to feel accepted by others. The people whose opinions matter most are called "significant others." Parents are usually the most powerful significant others.

Parents

It's almost impossible for parents to grasp how important they are in their children's lives. Their power within this arena is just awesome. In fact it may be argued that, in certain areas, parents have more control over their children's lives than they do over their own.

For our purposes, we will focus on how the parent-child relationship influences the development of humility. Though children do not possess humility, their childhood experiences do affect their adult personalities. Whether or not grown-ups develop humility depends, in large part, on their early experiences.

Where do children learn to compare themselves with each other? Why does competition seem so natural for kids? The answer is pretty clear—they learn from their parents. Parents are always comparing their kids. This is what supermarkets are for. They provide a central place where mothers can get together and compare their children. The time spent in the supermarket is directly proportional to how special a mother thinks her child is. The "gifted" child's parent will spend all afternoon in the grocery store hoping someone will ask, "How's Junior?" The delinquent's mother, on the other hand, flies in and out of the quick shop.

Fathers are just as bad. Take as an example the infamous Little League father. The Little League father doesn't understand why his son or daughter has to share the same field with those other nameless kids. He feels his child at least deserves a special uniform. The competition on the field is never as fierce as it is in the stands where fathers compete with other fathers through their children.

Too often parents get so caught up in the competition, they become blind to the best interests of the child. I once attended a Little League game where I watched a boy named Tim have a particularly difficult time. Tim went to the plate three times, but struck out each time without making any contact with the ball. In the outfield, Tim dropped a couple of routine pop-ups before being replaced. After the game, Tim's father tried to tell Tim how there are other things in life besides baseball. But the father ͜ and attitude belied his words. Tim knew his father wa͜ disappointed. Though he did not enjoy the game, Tim continued to try to play. For two more summers Tim tried and failed. Because of his awkwardness he was teased by other boys his age. After that first game, Tim's dad stayed home. Tim kept trying.

Tim wanted his father to be able to sit in the stands and be proud. He felt he had shamed his dad. I guess his dad was shamed but I don't feel sorry for this father. Poor Tim.

Some people spend their lives trying to please their parents. In many of these cases parental approval is held out like a carrot just beyond the person's reach. Acceptance is always contingent upon the successful completion of the *next* task. This sort of parent-child relationship produces one of life's most pathetic creatures—the perfectionist.

The perfectionist lives on a treadmill. He never seems to be able to quite reach his goal. Somewhere the perfectionist received the message that not only is perfection possible, it is necessary. Unfortunately, parents sometimes give this message to their children. They communicate that the child is acceptable only on the basis of what he achieves. This parent conveys the message, "I don't love you for who you are; I love you for what you can do."

The healthier parent conveys the message, "I love you for who you are *and* I love you for who you can become." In every healthy parent-child relationship there is an element of unconditional love. This love is based solely on the fact that the child exists. Unconditional love provides a solid foundation from which the child can risk, explore and grow. Striking out will not get exaggerated out of proportion. The child who feels genuinely loved does not risk parental rejection every time he steps up to the plate.

When the parent-child relationship is based on unconditional love, the child comes to realize that he does not have to
be perfect. He realizes that it's O.K. to have limitations. This
child accepts his potential because he is allowed to grow in
his own individual style.

The loving parent encourages growth, even though
growth leads to increased freedom. As the child grows, he
earns greater independence from parents and caretakers.
He develops a sense of self acceptance and self-sufficiency.
The most important ingredient required for self-acceptance
is the experience of being loved unconditionally. If the child
lives in such a relationship, the opportunity for a humble yet
proud acceptance of self awaits him.

Unconditional love does not mean that the child can do
as he pleases. Parents have the responsibility to provide
structure for their children. This involves making rules and
seeing to it that the children obey. A child's misbehavior
should bring immediate discipline. This discipline, however, should not include withdrawal of the parent's love.
The child should receive the message, "I discipline you
because I love you."

Children do not regulate their behavior to please
themselves. They shape their behavior to please their significant others. If children are accepted by the important
people in their lives, they are happy.

Children do not need humility in their lives. They have
no desire to accept themselves. Prior to adolescence, self-
acceptance is not a necessary trait. During the childhood
years, the child needs to be accepted by others. If this acceptance is not forthcoming then, as an adult, he may never be
able to accept himself. Without the childhood experience of
being loved for who you are, humility may forever elude
you.

Healthy Children

One of the best ways to evaluate a child's self-esteem is to observe him interacting with less fortunate children. Low self-esteem children will tease or belittle the handicapped and the retarded. They are also likely to be cruel to small animals. In this way they can demonstrate power and superiority. These kids see human limitation as weak points to be exploited.

The child with a healthy amount of self-esteem will have an easier time relating to a handicapped age-mate. The healthy child has enough of a conscience to know that every living being deserves respect. This child does not need to defeat everyone in order to be accepted by those he admires. If the child can accept shortcomings in other children, he is well on his way toward the eventual acceptance of his own limitations.

The child who grows up in a loving and caring environment where he experiences intimacy, encouragement and structure begins life in a place where life is celebrated. This environment is not created by wealth, high intelligence or political power. This situation develops when people who love and respect life come together.

When children feel secure, they unleash a tremendous curiosity. They ask questions which make adults tremble. Young children rarely accept the fact that there are some things we may never know. A first grade teacher once told me of an experience she had during art class. She was walking up the aisle examining the children's art work. She came across a little girl named Diane who was working feverishly on her project.

"What are you drawing?" asked the teacher.

"A picture of God," replied Diane.

"Oh . . . ," the teacher paused for a moment, "But no one knows what God looks like."

"When I'm finished this they will!" Diane stated confidently.

When I heard this story it was told as a funny. Though I laughed at the time, soon afterward I was bothered by a deeper message. I laughed at the child's foolishness and arrogance and later I recognized her wisdom. Diane drew God as she saw him. That's good enough. I admire the child's confidence in the face of the doubting teacher. I wonder if the second grade teacher or the third grade teacher finally broke her spirit. I hope not.

I don't think it's right to impose the limitations of reason on the dream of a child. The days of reason and logic lay awaiting the child in time. It is a mistake to consider the irrational nature of the child to be foolishness. Adults can learn a lot from kids. Children have a wisdom of their own. We are better off to let people young and old take full advantage of every stage of life.

Most adults do not believe in magic. Most children do. Adults feel that as children age, they realize that there is no magic. In my crazier moments, I wonder if we lose some magic when we stop believing. I shudder to think that the first grade teacher may have thrown away a genuine picture of God.

By the age of nine or ten, children come to understand that they cannot wish away life's difficult problems. At this point, they begin to understand that some things may not change at all. At this stage children realize that death is final and nothing can bring back the deceased. Reality is gaining power.

The disappearance of magical thinking can produce a crisis. The fat girl, the short boy, the stutterer and the "slow" child all begin to worry, a little more than before, about their futures. They may begin to feel more pessimistic. Anger, hostility or depression may appear. A sensitive adult can help a great deal by listening and giving accurate information concerning the young person's condition.

When pre-adolescents are faced with overwhelming problems, they may regress to the stage of magical thinking. They will use magic as a defense mechanism to wish away (or deny) their problems. Using magic, however, makes them passive observers. It keeps them from becoming actively involved in problem solving. Magic will also keep these young people from accepting the things they cannot change.

As the teenage years begin, the individual should feel a growing sense of significance. This is the feeling that one can create a future for oneself. People who never come to see themselves as responsible for their lives develop "the lottery syndrome." The lottery syndrome describes a limited behavioral repertoire which can do little more than hope for "good luck" (the adult term for magic). The only activity these people put forward is the effort required to buy a lottery ticket. They then sit back and hope and wait.

The lottery syndrome in some ways resembles drug addiction. The drug addict buys the drug, takes it and then sits back and waits. The output in terms of physical expenditure is minimal but the effects can be mind-shaking.

Another example of the lottery syndrome are those people who wait years in anticipation of a hefty inheritance. Instead of creating, they wait, sometimes for many years, for the opportunity to receive. In this case, the passive (or should I say lazy) son or daughter waits for the parent to die. Although there are no official statistics kept on this, I'm afraid this situation is all too common. Parents who breed lazy children should not be surprised to see them turn into vultures as death draws near.

The lottery syndrome represents a childish demand.

The affected person communicates, "I want something for nothing!" Not everyone who plays the lottery is affected by the lottery syndrome. The lottery syndrome describes people who live their lives in the same manner one would play the lottery, depending on luck and magic rather than work and skill.

It is difficult for the young person to let go of his belief in magic. With the absence of magic, he must accept his mortality. Mortality involves sickness, suffering and death. The limitations imposed by mortality, however, give structure to our lives. There is some consistency. We can make an honest appraisal of our limitations. These limitations define who we are.

The healthy child knows what it is like to be loved for who he is and for who he can be. This is not a contradiction. When a child feels loved for who he is, he feels secure. With this security he grows and develops in the direction of his talents. This growth is a natural occurrence once there is a secure foundation. The growth will continue as long as he is grounded in a secure relationship with parents or caretakers. Healthy parental love or "unconditional love" describes the relationship where the parent provides a secure relationship for the child and then encourages his growth.

The healthy child eventually learns to accept the fact that the best he can do is the best he can do. He delights in developing his potential. Though there may not yet be enough self-acceptance to tolerate major flaws in himself, he does have the security of knowing that certain important people (i.e. parents) will continue to love him in spite of his shortcomings.

Eventually the young person internalizes some of his parents' attitudes. If the parent accepts the child for who he is, the child will be much more likely to accept himself. If the parents encourage growth, the growing child will begin to reinforce himself for his accomplishments. The loving parent-child relationship also serves to give the child a deep appreciation of people. As the child enters adolescence, he moves further away, physically, from his parents. What he has internalized, however, stays with him like a guardian angel.

During adolescence, reality continues to gain power. The teenager's greatest fear is a return to the dependency of childhood. His second greatest fear is the fear of the adult world. The teenager lives in heaven, hell and limbo all at the same time. During this, the most self-conscious time of life, the teen lives to be recognized as someone special. In early adolescence, he separated himself from his family; in mid-adolescence he wants to feel unique amongst his age-mates.

Years 13 to 18 can be described as the best of times and the worst of times. Mood swings are common. When the teenager is reinforced in his independence, he will feel wonderful. The fear of adulthood gives way to a newfound confidence. When he is rejected in his fragile identity, he feels the pains of hell. The setback is likely to be exaggerated. He may feel humiliated if he is turned down for a date.

Between these ups and downs there are usually periods where "everything's cool." These are times to practice some conformity as well as do some low key experimentation on one's identity. During these times the teenager will watch to see how others handle particular situations.

When adolescents attempt major experimentation with their identities, like piercing their noses, they usually do so by the slogan, "You're only young once!" This cliche seems to validate the theory that youth is a time to try new things. Ironically, when kids attempt things with the motivation from—"You're only young once!"—they usually age.

Some teenagers live with the attitude, "Live it up now for

tomorrow we may die!" Sometimes this is translated into, "Is there life after high school?" What these teens don't realize is that adolescence does not have to end. Lots of people stay adolescents well past middle age. To hold on to adolescence, one must postpone all decisions and commitments which are part of the adult world. Relationships must remain free and nonbinding. Financial support must come from parents or from jobs which do not require commitments. The adolescent never develops a career.

The ultimate criterion for remaining in adolescence concerns the individual's self-esteem. The child develops his self-esteem primarily on the basis of how parents and authorities act toward him. The adolescent's level of self-esteem is controlled by the acceptance he receives from his peers. The adult, however, maintains a degree of self-esteem and self-respect which is independent of his context. The adult accepts himself.

If an individual cannot accept himself, he has not completed adolescence. As long as his opinion of himself is controlled solely by what other people think, he cannot enter adulthood. Without some self-acceptance he is not ready to make his own decisions. Nor is he ready to make any kind of commitment.

Why does someone remain dependent on the evaluation of others? All the possible answers to this question could fill volumes. Most of these answers, I believe, would reflect a common theme. When a person cannot accept himself, he becomes dependent on the acceptance of others. Acceptance from others can assuage feelings of inferiority. If such a person is rejected by others, he has very little left. He now feels unacceptable to himself and others. Without a certain degree of acceptance from someone (anyone), the individual is likely to become cruel to himself, others or both.

By the end of adolescence people make an important

decision. We decide how we will actively relate to our world. Our emphasis is no longer on how well the world will treat us. As young adults we realize that we can shape our world. We usually decide to treat the world in the same fashion we have been treated. If the young adult feels accepted by family and friends for who he is, he will probably make a sincere attempt to accept himself and his world.

Conclusion

The single most important ingredient required for self-acceptance is the experience of being loved unconditionally. The feeling of being genuinely loved for who we are, flaws and all, serves as an anchor in our minds and our hearts. The memory never dies. Psychologist Irving Yalom has written that "the experience of intimacy is permanent. It can never be taken away. It exists in one's inner world as a permanent reference point: a reminder of one's potential for intimacy. The discovery of self that ensues as a result of intimacy is also permanent."[2] Hopefully this memory is firmly in place by the time adolescence begins.

After a child has experienced being accepted by others, he can move toward accepting the people in his world. As he develops a respect and appreciation for his fellow beings, he will begin to accept himself. At this point, a very healthy cycle begins. The more we accept others, the more we will accept ourselves. The more we accept ourselves, the more we will accept others.

CHAPTER FOUR

Adults

The greatest fault of all is to be conscious of none.
— Thomas Carlyle

In chapters one and two I discussed how humility can add to the life of an adult. In this chapter I will attend to specific aspects of the adult world which can be drastically affected by the presence or absence of humility.

As time passes, people develop a greater need for humility. We come to realize the limits of our magic. Though we may experience an occasional miracle, we eventually realize that we are not creating the miracles. Graceful aging requires that we develop the courage to accept difficult things we cannot change.

Sex

When I was a kid, my mother used to say she knew God has a sense of humor because only someone with a sense of humor would make a giraffe. At the time this seemed perfectly logical. When I reached adulthood, however, I came to my own conclusions. I realized that God has a sense of humor because only someone with a sense of humor could create sex.

Sex is one of those things animals, even giraffes, do better than people. People work at it; animals just do it. To animals, sex is a pleasurable experience which also (whether they know it or not) propagates the species. Sex is a natural phenomenon which causes little shame or embarrassment in the animal kingdom. Animals have the audacity to copulate on the roadside, on the lawn, and even when surrounded by their peers, their owners and the neighbor's kids. In fact, I think that children serve as aphrodisiacs for many animals. Why else would monkeys begin making love as soon as a 3rd grade class approaches?

Humans, however, take sex much more seriously because we risk so much more. We so often believe that sexual problems are humiliations. Sexual failure is worse than sexual perversion. The fact that someone else is there to see the failure multiplies the embarrassment. Men, for example, would not have nearly as much trouble living with occasional impotence if only it did not have to occur in front of a woman.

When sexual problems arise, the individual's shame can cause one to lose trust in one's partner. The impotent man fears that his wife will tell her best friend or her therapist who in turn will tell someone else and so on and so on until everyone including his boss and bowling team knows that he is having "that kind of a problem." When the trust in a relationship begins to break down, the real problems start. Transient episodes of impotence occur in 50% of the male population.[1] An occasional bout with impotence is no cause for shame. We are entitled to our flaws, even our sexual ones.

Even when there are no "problems" people are often

ashamed of their sexuality. First we are ashamed of our inexperience and then of our aging bodies. I think one reason many people insist on fidelity from their partners is to prevent comparisons with other people's sexual performances. Underneath the surface lives a fear that everyone else can do "it" better than me.

What is so ridiculous about sex is that we've taken a natural experience and turned it into a game show. It is so easy to get caught up in the statistics which say how much, how many, how loud and how daring. Animals have sex while physically surrounded by other animals. Many people have sex with the same feeling. They feel that their performances are being monitored by the world. These people usually feel that their skills are just not good enough.

Group pressure should not decide what makes a healthy sexual relationship. Healthy sex is defined by the two people in the relationship. The healthy sexual relationship provides for the needs of the people involved in the experience. When their needs are met, the experience is perfect enough. It doesn't matter how long or how many times "most people" have sex. All that matters are the two individuals.

Sexual hang-ups are rooted in the feeling that one is not "good enough." Ever since Adam and Eve discovered fig leaves, humans have been plagued with feelings of sexual inadequacy. We have difficulty understanding that the only standards we have to live up to are those produced in our intimate relationships. We don't have to try to satisfy the world.

Minor problems become major ones when we punish ourselves for having minor problems. Nowhere is this more evident than in the arena we call sexuality. Throughout this book I have been saying that the healthy and mature individual accepts himself for what he is and for what he can be.

Likewise a healthy relationship can accept itself for what it is—Not Perfect. In fact sharing imperfection can spawn greater intimacy.

Marriage and Divorce

I recently heard that a divorce occurs every 27 seconds in the United States. After I heard that statement, I waited about thirty seconds and then wondered about the newest divorced couple. What were they like? Were there children? Were they glad to get it over with? Was either person hurt badly?

I soon realized that if I went through this every thirty seconds I'd be an emotional wreck. My only chance to save my sanity was to divert my attention. Before doing so, however, I had to put my thoughts together on the subject.

People do not stay married because they love each other. Couples stay married because they need each other. Happy marriages are based on love but not all marriages are happy ones. Many couples stay together long after the fire has died. They do so because they believe that, for one of a number of reasons, they are still better off than they would be if they were divorced. Divorce is not the only way to fail at marriage. People who fail at their marriage often stay together.

When people come to realize that they need something, they are exercising humility. To say "I need something" implies that I am not completely self-sufficient. The individual who will not acknowledge his need for other people is not a good candidate for marriage. These people get married for fun. They stay together as long as the good times last. When they divorce, they try to communicate to the world, "I don't need anyone." When this facade begins to break, loneliness slips through the cracks.

In healthy marriages, spouses acknowledge that they love and need each other not only because they need people in general, but also because they love and need the individual qualities of their spouse. Certain people complement the talents of certain others. The right relationship can help vitalize the potential of both spouses.

It's a shame that so many people get married just for the sake of being married. These people usually do so in a desperate attempt to cure loneliness or bolster self-esteem. They feel that all they need is someone, anyone. Such people lack an accurate description of what they need in a relationship. They need the humility to honestly and courageously face themselves. They need to ask themselves, "What do I *specifically* need in a relationship?

Humble people realize that no one is perfect. When they enter relationships, they are not looking for perfection. They can accept certain faults in their loved ones. In the counseling process, I often ask clients, "What faults are you able to tolerate in a friend?" This question usually surprises people. Sometimes people feel that they are the only ones who are not perfect.

The dating process serves as a time to get to know yourself and your partner. It is not possible to make a commitment to someone until you know that person. Nor is it possible to commit yourself until you know yourself. In the security of a growing relationship, one feels a little safer to expose one's real self. When the real self emerges, we are ready to make mature decisions and lasting commitments.

Without humility, we could not admit to having needs. We would only be able to face the "good" things about ourselves. If we only face the good in ourselves, we do not know ourselves. If we only express the enviable aspects of being, we will remain unknown to our friends, our children and our husbands and wives. People who bottle up aspects of their being develop feelings of loneliness. They live with the knowledge that "people don't know the real me."

When spouses no longer feel the need for each other, they seek a divorce. Through the divorce process, the individual comes to realize the mortality of dreams and the frailty of aspirations. The dream which began with ". . . and they lived happily ever after" now ends with a painful awakening. Fear increases as the individual sees that life does not have the predictability he once thought. The individual often feels that somewhere in life he made a terrible mistake. But where? "Maybe we should never have gotten married? Maybe we did too many things wrong during the marriage? Maybe we're making a mistake by getting a divorce? Maybe we should keep working at it?"

"Somewhere a mistake was made. But where?" The answer to this question, unfortunately, may be unattainable. Even hindsight can be impaired. But just facing the fact that one has made a mistake can be a tremendous lesson. Learning that one is fallible adds maturity to all future decisions. Many people pay a severe price for this lesson.

Mistakes need not shatter one's confidence. Hopefully, however, they will remedy one's arrogance. The wise person realizes that fallibility characterizes humanity. Decisions are made with care and deliberation only when we accept the fact that mistakes are possible. If we are infallible, there would be no need to think.

The decision to remarry will depend on how well the individual learns from experience. People who cannot function outside of wedlock are likely to jump into "rebound marriages." These folks search for any port in a storm. Their mate selection is more or less incidental. They just want to be married again. The rebound marriage occurs when the divorced person does not take the time to understand what happened in the previous marriage. This produces an insecure and divided self.

People avoid examining themselves and their experience if they feel they cannot handle what they might find. The fear of flaws causes more ignorance than laziness. We can learn from our experience only if we face our lives—past and present. Socrates said the unexamined life is not worth living. Socrates was by no means a pessimist. The unexamined life is a life out of control.

Careers

When I ask myself, "What am I?" the first thing that comes to my mind is my job—therapist. If I think a while longer, I come up with "husband and father." It's a simple question which doesn't conjure up much anxiety. When I ask myself, "Who am I?", however, I tremble. I then find myself trying to return to the question, "What am I?"— Indeed, "What am I?" often precludes the question "Who am I?" Certainly "What am I?" is an easier question to answer.

"What am I?" and "Who am I?" are two different questions. When the two are intertwined, people answer "Who am I?" in terms of doctor, lawyer or Indian chief. This results in an extremely shallow understanding of oneself.

People identify themselves solely in terms of careers for several reasons. A career can give a person a tremendous amount of power and prestige. The policeman can carry a gun. The physician can write prescriptions. A therapist can help people change life styles. An artist can create new forms. A priest can forgive sins. An educator can shape attitudes. Each career has special privileges.

A partial definition of "identity" could be "one's unique

arrangement of special talents." A large part of who I am relates to what I can do. But there is much more. To fully grasp who I am, I also need to know what I cannot do. So to complete the definition of human identity we can say, "Identity reflects one's unique arrangement of special talents and special limitations."

A job title represents something the individual can do. As such, it serves as an answer to the question, "What are you?" We should keep in mind that the person who asks, "What are you?" is usually a stranger. Consequently, it may be appropriate to say only what one does for a living. This is O.K. as long as we remember that there is a difference between "what" I am and "who" I am. When searching for "who" I am, I am looking for both my talents and my limitations.

Another reason for asking only "what" I am relates to this question's simplicity. Except while unemployed, we always know what we are. Unemployment would be our only identity crisis. When we ask "what," we can answer with a single simple dimension.

Basing our identities totally on our careers, however, produces a very restricted view of ourselves. If I never face the deeper question, "Who am I?", I will never know who I am. When a person comes for counseling, it is important that he (eventually) be willing to consider the question, "Who am I?" Human beings develop feelings of guilt, restlessness and severe boredom when we restrict our potential. All work and nothing else makes people (even successful workers) miserable.

The medical profession provides us with an interesting example. Many physicians work under a great deal of stress. They feel pressure to perform well (sometimes asked to perform miracles), and they are frequently surrounded by death and suffering. These conditions can take a terrible toll on a person. The medical profession is rapidly becoming aware of the problem. Within this profession, there is an alarming rate of alcoholism, drug abuse and suicide.

In an attempt to treat this situation, the medical profession has created a curious clinical entity called "the impaired physician." The term "impaired physician" is a euphemism which tries to make the problem of physicians sound special. Being an "impaired physician" is an elite affliction. Unfortunately, the concept of the impaired physician only makes matters worse.

A person who practices medicine for a living and who runs into psychological and emotional problems cannot be helped as long as he considers himself an impaired physician. He needs to understand himself as a human being with a problem. Life involves more than his career. If his career responsibilities control all his time and energy, then a tremendous amount of potential will be wasted. He will never develop new aspects of his being. Many physicians develop emotional problems because they cannot escape the pressures of their work. To treat such men and women as "impaired physicians" rather than "human beings" (like everyone else) only serves to perpetuate their entrapment. People cannot understand themselves solely on the basis of their careers. There is so much more to people.

During our working years, our career responsibilities have a high priority. But we must never forget that there are other dimensions to our being. Without a personal life, we risk losing individual uniqueness and style. Our life force is our curiosity. When we look in only one direction, our curiosity dies. When curiosity dies, boredom and then cruelty ensue. Our careers provide only one direction. People need to look around.

Public Speakers

Have you ever noticed that the less someone has to say, the longer it takes them to say it? Why can't more people be honest? Why can't they just say, "I don't know?" I guess some of humility's greatest enemies are soapboxes, microphones and audiences.

Jealousy

Jealousy fills the lives of those who feel unlovable. We cannot accept ourselves if we feel unlovable. The unlovable person is an angry person until a sense of helplessness sets in. People who feel unlovable usually try to force others to love them before they finally give up. While they are angry, they typically direct their hostility toward anyone who threatens their marginal self-esteem. Since their self-esteem is so frail, many things threaten it.

People are rarely jealous of animals, plants or inanimate objects. This is because the jealous person cannot get what he needs from animals or objects. Instead he makes demands on other people. He demands to be loved. He resents anyone who threatens to prevent love and acceptance from coming his way. The jealous person resents people who appear to be "better" because they make him look "worse." Again we see low self-esteem spawning a competitive life style.

Severe jealousy cannot be remedied by humility alone. Intense jealousy is rooted in the feeling of being unlovable. Nothing can help a person accept himself while he feels unlovable. If we see ourselves as unlovable, we see ourselves as unacceptable to ourselves and others. The only hope for the intensely jealous individual is for him to experience a relationship where he feels genuinely understood and accepted.

The petty jealousies which plague so many of us, however, are the direct result of a lack of humility. Try the following. Make a list of things you do not, and probably never will, do well. How many of these can you accept? How many of these things upset you? Now suppose your neighbor is very good at something you cannot do well but thought you could accept. How do you feel now?

There is a difference between accepting a limitation (humility) and trying to forget a limitation (repression). When you have the humility to accept your own shortcomings, you can live with the fact that there are other people who can do what you cannot. When you try to force your flaws from your awareness, however, you resent anyone who invites these undesirable entities into consciousness. This resentment constitutes petty jealousy.

Jealousy represents the projection of our disappointment in ourselves. If we cannot accept our flaws, we will be jealous of anyone who reminds us of these shortcomings. Jealous people feel their limitations are magnified by the presence of others who are not similarly flawed. The amount of humility we possess is indirectly proportional to our jealousy—the less humility, the more jealousy.

Gratitude

What does it take to say "thank you?" What do we mean when we thank someone? What does "you're welcome" mean? When we express our appreciation, we are making a statement about ourselves. But what are we saying? Are we expressing indebtedness? And when the other person says "you're welcome," does that mean that the debt is cleared?

Let's suppose that the words "thank you" and "you're welcome" were removed from the English language. Instead of assuming that everyone knew the meaning of these terms, we would now have to explain exactly what we mean. If you could not say "thank you," what would you say to the person who found your wallet and returned it intact? What would you say to the person who gave you a gift, patted you on the back, or helped find your lost child?

I'm not suggesting that we remove "thank you" from the language. But I am suggesting that we sometimes use this term to hide our true feelings. Sometimes the phrase "thank you" is just not enough. Sometimes we need to do more than just be polite.

When we say "thank you" to someone we are acknowledging our need for that person. That individual has made us happier, healthier or safer. Because a "thank you" acknowledges a need, it is based in humility. It takes humility to say "thank you." That's why children are always forgetting to say it. Children have very little humility. When children say "thank you," they usually do so because they feel that it is what they are supposed to say.

Adults sometimes say "thank you" for the very same reason. We say it because we are supposed to, rather than to express our sincere gratitude. If we could no longer say "thank you," maybe we would never express any gratitude. But I don't think so. I think we would begin to more clearly articulate our gratitude and appreciation if we would not hide behind the trite formality of "thank you, you're welcome." And that's exactly what it has become—a trite formality.

A trite insincere "thank you" does not require much humility. This type of gratitude dies as soon as it hears "you're welcome" or "forget it." This empty ritual is merely an attempt to conform with protocol.

So who is the worse for the shallow expression of gratitude? The answer—everyone who hides their unique feelings and/or foregoes the individual expression of these feelings. The feeling of sincere gratitude is an important humbling experience. The expression of this feeling adds to and deepens the experience. If we lose touch with this feeling, by refusing to honestly express it, we run the risk of becoming arrogant. We may conclude that we do not need anyone for anything. Without feelings of gratitude and appreciation, we may become incapable of love.

Poets and romantics have described the heart as the symbol of human love. Just about everyone recognizes this symbol. Using the heart as the symbol of love, the question comes to mind, "What is the heart made of?" I suppose many people have opinions on this. So do I. I think the heart is made up of a list. This list contains all the sincere "thank you's" and "you're welcome's" one has expressed in one's lifetime. Every time we express genuine appreciation, the heart grows bigger and warmer. With each sincere "you're welcome" we convey in our own individual style after helping someone, the heart deepens. The size of the heart depends on the amount of kindness and gratitude it holds.

The relationship between love and gratitude can also be seen in another arena. Often the feeling "I love you" is very similar to the feeling of intense gratitude. It's like, "I love you because you've done so much for me." I don't think we could love someone if we didn't allow ourselves to experience gratitude.

Cosmetic Surgery

Due to the so-called miracles of modern science, we can now change most areas of our appearance. As time goes by, more and more people are having their faces lifted, noses shortened, hair transplanted and breasts enlarged. There is also a growing legion of folks who are in serious conflict concerning whether or not they should go such a route. Most of these people worry that their face lift or whatever will be a demonstration of vanity. They feel that they will be humiliated because of this vanity.

If a "nose job" or a face lift makes a person feel better about themselves, then where is the problem? If no one gets hurt, then where is the crime? There is no need to exaggerate this point out of proportion. A nose is a nose. If yours is too long you can have it shortened. But don't pretend that a short nose or a full head of hair or a tight face is the answer to all of life's problems. That would be vanity.

When I was in school I knew a girl who had what is sometimes called a "hook nose." She was very shy and yet those few people who really got to know her found her to be a wonderful person. Then suddenly, after returning from Christmas break, she had a new nose. She had it fixed, and with it, there was a tremendous change in her personality. Almost overnight she became confident and outgoing.

In the weeks that followed, it seems as though she was a perfect example of the wonders of cosmetic surgery. She really seemed happy. She now had the attention of many young men. But she did not live happily ever after. She could not change her life as quickly as the surgeons changed her nose. Her new relationships with boys did not turn out to be all she hoped for. She was hurt very badly. I don't know how the story ended. I hope she adjusted O.K.

It is healthy to take pride in one's appearance. Removing a stain or a wart from one's face can hardly be considered vanity. Vanity occurs when we dwell on our outer appearance at the cost of ignoring our inner being. In this case, looks become more important than feelings. Time, money and energy are spent in an attempt to perfect the facade rather than settle the inner conflict or the conflict between people.

If looking good helps a person feel good about himself and the world he lives in, then improving his appearance is a small, yet positive step. But no one should make the mistake of believing that a shorter nose or smaller buttocks will solve all of one's problems.

The Search for Perfection

I have been trying my best to ridicule the popular myth of human perfection. We all repeat the worn out phrase, "Nobody's perfect," but what many people really mean is, "Nobody's perfect, but I have to be." This makes for a life filled with frustration. The problem stems from the fact that we can experience perfection, and yet we cannot create perfect lives for ourselves. Life seems to tease us with occasional encounters with perfection. When we try to capture these moments in anything but our memories, they disappear.

We can experience perfect moments. With a little luck, we can experience a perfect afternoon or even a perfect day. To increase our chances of attaining some perfection, societies create situations called games where we can experience brief moments of perfection. In baseball a pitcher can throw a "perfect game," a golfer can hit a hole-in-one, and a bowler can bowl a 300 game. Clearly, our fleeting moments of perfection are truly enjoyable.

These moments are so pleasurable that we become tempted to strive for constant perfection. Here is where problems arise. Searching for the perfect life serves as an excuse to run away from reality. Searching for perfection sounds good but it belies one's true intentions. The perfect life is a mirage. And deep inside we all know it is a mirage.

The person who looks for a perfect career does not want to work. The individual who seeks a perfect marriage really wants to stay single. If we ate only perfect meals we would starve. The search for a perfect life is an insidious game.

Insecure parents who cannot bear to grant their sons and daughters the freedoms of adulthood will frequently play this game. They give the children their blessings to marry on the condition that they find a perfect spouse. On the surface this seems like loving concern. But since the parents know, either consciously or unconsciously, that no such being exists, what appears to be loving concern is really an insecure form of attachment.

The quest for the perfect life is similar to the search for leprechauns, wizards, gnomes or the fountain of youth. It would be nice to find any one of these things but they just don't seem to exist. Fortunately, none of these are necessary to find happiness. Can you imagine what it would be like if we couldn't be happy until we found a gnome or a leprechaun? Isn't it a shame that so many people think they have to be perfect in order to be happy?

Despair

If we are to live life to the fullest we must face the good and the bad—the hugs and the slugs. The hard times can make us strong. Without misery we would not appreciate joy. Throughout history, people have demonstrated the tendency to place great value on things that are not easily attainable. Hence the tremendous demand for gold, diamonds, rainbows and miracles. Rainbows, for example, are appreciated not only for their beauty per se but because they symbolize an end to clouds and rain. In the same manner, our joy and happiness are enriched by the knowledge that we have survived sorrow.

Despair describes the depths of human sorrow. Despair is never a pleasant experience and yet it can add to our pleasant experiences. Surviving despair can give us a feeling of strength and confidence as well as add to our appreciation of the good times.

Despair, however, can do more for us than help us appreciate our happy times. Despair is part of a tremendously important learning process. Many aspects of life are difficult to accept, and our encounters with the tragic dimensions of life may lead to despair. While in despair, we struggle to come to terms with things that hurt. The feeling that we will never again know or feel anything but despair creates a feeling of entrapment. While in the depths of despair we feel overwhelmed. During this time, we face things which previously we were able to avoid, things like our imperfections and our inability to completely control our destinies.

Despair can be an important point in personal change. Alcoholics Anonymous believes that the alcoholic can only begin to recover once he "hits bottom." This is the point of total despair. Here the person takes a good hard look at the stark realities of his life. Denial is now completely shattered and the individual clearly sees himself and the world he helped create. Many mental health professionals feel that once someone has reached the point of complete despair he has three alternatives: 1) suicide, 2) insanity or 3) dedicate himself to treatment. Only the individual can make this decision. At this point the person can end his life or try to rebuild it. If he can survive despair, he can change his life. "After despair, the one thing left is possibility."[2]

Despair can be an important part of the therapeutic process. It can signal the point where the client has dropped his facade and has begun to examine his real self. According to Rollo May:

Authentic despair is that emotion which forces one to
come to terms with one's destiny. It is the great enemy
of pretense, the foe of playing ostrich. It is a demand to
face the reality of one's life.[3]

The individual who designs his life to avoid despair will
have to restrict his reality to the point where he can see only
the pleasantries. This person frequently abuses alcohol and/
or drugs. These drugs are often prescribed by well-
intentioned physicians who do not understand the value of
the feelings which their patients describe as painful. Physicians, for example, will sometimes medicate a patient in
order to suppress the despair which comes with grief and
bereavement. Unfortunately, such a procedure frequently
complicates and impedes the grieving process. Feelings of
grief need to be faced and worked through.

If we want to experience reality clearly, we need to open
ourselves up to all emotions. If we fear certain emotions, we
will fear certain realities. To repress an emotion means we
must avoid the aspects of our reality which trigger that
feeling. Rollo May encourages therapists to allow their
clients to experience despair:

There are some misguided therapists who feel that
they must reassure the patient at every point of despair. But if the client never feels despair, it is doubtful
whether he will ever feel any profound emotion.[4]

Living life to the fullest means touching all the textures,
looking at all the colors, listening to all the sounds, tasting all
the flavors and feeling all the feelings. Our emotions are our
inner responses to the reality we perceive. If we do not
permit ourselves to experience sorrow and despair, we will
have to avoid the painful dimensions of our being. We will

consistently attempt to ignore our limitations and imperfections.

Getting to know ourselves and our world requires that we encounter the good and the not-so-good. With each encounter there is an emotional response. All human emotion can be used appropriately during the course of our lives. If we allow ourselves to accept even the most painful emotions into our lives, we will experience a much greater reality.

Aging

The single greatest untapped resource in the world is our elderly. Our society thinks of the elderly in terms of what they no longer have. Seldom do we fully appreciate the talents they may have acquired through their experiences. So many of us see old age as the absence of youth rather than an important stage of life in its own right. The wisdom which comes with age is seen as a small consolation prize. Who cares if you're wiser if you can't play an intense game of tennis? Who cares about wisdom if you can't remember your social security number? The accent is always on "you can't."

Perhaps the primary reason we have difficulty relating to the elderly is the fact that when we do we are looking at our own features. We see that one day we will slow down and become vulnerable to illness, criminals and prejudice. Life is the story to which we do not want to know the ending.

Growing old means facing painful aspects of reality. One of the most dramatic personal events that occurs during adulthood is a shift in time perspective, when one starts thinking in terms of time-left-to-live rather than time-since-birth.[5] As adults age, emotional health demands that one's mortality be accepted and incorporated into one's life style. This represents one of the major tasks of adult development. Ironically, when elderly adults finally accept death—accept it to the point where they can talk and even joke about it—the younger people in their world write them off as being senile.

In order for our society to appreciate the talents of the elderly, we have to honestly face that portion of our population. We need to face the elderly. We also need to face ourselves. We lose certain freedoms as our lives progress. This is a condition of life. If we can accept this, we may get close enough to the aged to see the treasure.

Few people enthusiastically wait for old age. The gains never seem to equal the losses. How would you answer the question, "What are the advantages of old age?" For many people this is a difficult question to answer. But when we ask, "What are the disadvantages of old age?", answers spring to mind immediately. So let's focus on the former.

We learn from experience. The more extensive our range of experience, the greater our store of knowledge. Knowledge turns to wisdom as the elderly person accepts and integrates his experience. As one weaves these lessons together he comes to an understanding of life. The older person will integrate and synthesize experience rather than disect and analyze as younger adults do. This ability to face life is directly related to the development of humility.

More than any other time in his life, the old person is faced with his human limitations. The body has a will of its own; it slows down and weakens. In order for an old person to continue to avoid his weaknesses, he must retreat into a reduced reality. This means closing his mind to many conditions of his existence. This state of being is usually called senility. In many cases, the "senile" individual will continue to focus exclusively on memories of his youth rather than accept and deal with his present circumstances.

Contrary to popular belief, however, the majority of old

people do not flee from reality in an attempt to preserve their youth. In fact, older adults are less inclined than younger ones to use escapist fantasy as a means of defense against the stresses of life.[6]

The wisdom and humility we develop while we age are necessary to accomplish the most important tasks of our final years. The elderly need the humility to face all the dimensions of their being. They need to contemplate their past, their present and their fate (death). Along with the humility to accept their lives, many old people possess the wisdom to integrate this wide array of experiences and come to an understanding of life. We cannot understand life until we accept it. We cannot understand people until we accept them. In the same manner, we cannot understand ourselves until we accept ourselves. Before we honestly explore anything, we need to accept the fact that what we find may be painful. If people develop humility, I believe we can find the meaning to our lives before we die.

The final task of a full life is to find meaning in one's life. What did I do with my time? Why? Can I accept my life or am I too ashamed? Before dying, most people have the opportunity to conduct their own review and evaluation. It's interesting that many religions teach that after one's life is finished, God reviews that life and decides how acceptable it has been. For people who adhere to this belief, an acceptance of one's life leads to an acceptance of death. A life which is acceptable to the individual is usually a life one believes will be acceptable to God. It is very difficult for a religious person to accept himself if he feels that he is not acceptable to God. Consequently, the belief in a forgiving God can greatly aid in the acceptance of self.

The wise and humble old person leaves this world knowing he is flawed and yet feeling no shame.

Spirituality

There are more things in the universe than we can see. Our eyes cannot reach all that exists. We develop a certain wisdom when we accept this.

Yet the world we see can itself be overwhelming. It is so expansive, so confusing, so awesome. We live with the temptation to restrict the size of our universe. We try to convince ourselves that something exists only if we can confirm it through sight or touch. We call this the "scientific approach."

But if the only things which exist are the things we can see and touch, then science has no future. There would be nothing left to discover.

Science does not close off dimensions of our universe, we do. We are responsible for ourselves. Fear and arrogance keep us from looking beyond ourselves. When this occurs our spiritual dimension starves.

Samuel Dresner once said that the greatest consequence of arrogance, and ultimately its most disastrous effect, is spiritual blindness:

> When our own ego is the constant center of all our concern, decisions and actions, and when our own selves are the shining hub in which are set the numberless spokes of life, around which all our thoughts, feelings and encounters revolve in a never changing whirl of self-centeredness, then we have blinders over our spiritual eyes.[7]

Arrogance obstructs our vision of God. If the arrogant person sees God at all, it is usually in the form of a gift giver, a force which rewards the person for his goodness. Likewise, the person who feels inferior, if he sees God at all, tends to see Him as a judge who only serves to punish.

Should arrogance and inferiority wane, the struggle for spiritual development can begin. Bill W. described this phenomenon in A.A. members:

> For just so long as we were convinced that we could live exclusively by our own individual strength and intelligence, for just that long was a working faith in a Higher Power impossible.
>
> This was true even when we believed that God existed. We could actually have earnest religious beliefs which remained barren because we were still trying to play God ourselves. As long as we placed self-reliance first, a genuine reliance upon a Higher Power was out of the question.[8]

True humility and an open mind can lead us to faith.[9] It is hard to come to terms with things which are difficult to understand. Struggling with confusion is a humbling experience which too many people avoid. Yet by working through this experience, we can find God as well as deeper layers of ourselves.

Some people are afraid to expand their horizons because they feel that a larger universe makes them even smaller. They feel that the presence of a Higher Power makes them an even lower power. These people are threatened by anything more powerful than they are. They feel that a reliance on God is a sign of weakness rather than a source of strength.

In the book *Twelve Steps and Twelve Traditions*, the co-founder of A.A. writes, "During the process of learning more about humility, the most profound result of all was the change in our attitude toward God."[10] Humility allows one to develop a mature spirituality. Only when we can accept that there is more to the universe than what meets our imperfect eyes can we begin to understand God.

Until we develop humility we cannot accept our place in the universe or genuinely accept the presence of a Higher Power. We feel God is a threat to us only when our own humanity threatens us. If I can accept who I am, in spite of my imperfection, I am ready to present myself to God.

Of all the tragedies which result from our neglect of humility, this may be the most severe. On the road to a healthy spirituality we encounter humility. If we learn humility we can move on to a greater understanding of God and our world. If we do not grow into humility, our sojourn ends. The door to humility is the point where so many of us end our journey in life. We encounter this unfamiliar state and then retreat never to grow any further.

So now we move on in our consideration of humility. As this state becomes better understood, and hence less anxiety provoking, we will be better prepared to move into the realm which lies beyond humility—namely spirituality.

CHAPTER FIVE

Death

Once you accept your own death all of a sudden you are free to live. You no longer care about your reputation . . . you no longer care except so far as your life can be used tactically—to promote a cause you believe in.
　　　　　　　　　　　　　　　— Saul Alinsky

The more complete one's life is, the more . . . one's creative capacities are fulfilled, the less one fears death. . . . People are not afraid of death per se, but of the incompleteness of their lives.
　　　　　　　　　　　　　— Lisl Marburg Goodman

Humility describes the ability to recognize and accept the limitations of our lives. There is no greater limitation to our being than death. Death limits our lives and the lives of our loved ones. In order to understand what we have to work with in life, we need to consider death.

In the earlier chapters, I discussed the fact that our society has not paid much attention to the virtue humility. There is not much fame and glory that come with accepting yourself and your world. I believe there is a connection between this and the fact that we are also a death denying culture. We, as a society, do our best to avoid any confrontations with human limitations such as death. We really believe that ignorance is bliss.

The denial of death seems to start in childhood. Most parents avoid discussing death with their children because they feel that kids aren't ready to listen. Children, on the other hand, do not verbalize their questions about death because they know their parents are afraid of the subject. Raised in such an environment, children gradually learn to fear death. Younger children do not fear death. The fear of death is not innate. It is a learned phenomenon.

Children come to see death as a monster which separates them from the people they need and love. The child's greatest fear is isolation. To the child, being "dead" is not so bad, but being left alone is pure terror. Consequently, bereaved children will frequently contemplate, and even attempt, suicide in an effort to be reunited with their lost loved ones. Death does not scare them as much as their isolation and loneliness.

Many adults fear death for a similar reason. We fear death because of what our death might do to our loved ones. It is common to hear of adults who, when faced with the possibility of dying, think only of their spouses and children. The adult, as opposed to the child, is more likely to fear death for what it might do to his loved ones. Yet both the child and the adult are capable of valuing someone else's life more than their own.

We face death on two fronts. We live with the fact that death can take us away at any time. We also live with the knowledge that death can rob us of the people we love. Of the two, I believe it is harder for most people to accept the latter.

We will now examine the human struggle to accept death. First we will look at the acceptance of our own mortality. Then we will consider how one goes about accepting the loss of a loved one.

Accepting our Mortality

While I was in graduate school, I spent a year and a half doing research on the psychological effects of heart attack. It was my first experience with people who were so close to death. For most of the people in my study, this was the first time they looked directly at the possibility of their own deaths.

Shortly after I began to interview these patients, I realized that something was wrong. I was interested in death but I was not comfortable talking about it. This was not supposed to be a problem because, in order to do my research, the hospital forbade me from talking about death. My interviews were supposed to focus solely on "getting better."

Many of the patients I spoke with, however, clearly conveyed a need to discuss their lives and their deaths. For instance, not too far into my research, I encountered a patient whom I will call Mr. Jason. Mr. Jason was only in his early fifties and yet he had a long history of severe heart trouble. Before I met with him, his cardiologist told me that Mr. Jason would probably die within the next week or so. For Mr. Jason, there would be no getting better.

During the next seven days I developed a friendship and a deep respect for Mr. Jason. He was honest and serene with large muscular arms and a soft handshake. I knew he was dying and yet I did not fear for him. He somehow convinced me that everything was O.K. He seemed to accept death with a tear and a smile.

One afternoon I sat with Mr. Jason in front of a large picture window on the tenth floor of the hospital. For almost two hours we sat looking out into mid-summer St. Louis. He talked and I listened. He spoke of his life growing up and then raising children in the inner city. He talked about parties and friends. But I can't really remember much of what he told me—it was the way he talked that had the greatest impact.

I could not identify his feelings at first. For a moment I thought he had lost his feelings. Then I realized that he had no one particular feeling that I could put a handle on. It seemed that he was expressing all human feelings. All his feelings had equal strength. All his feelings were alive.

As the sun began to set, I began to feel a profound change in my own being. Like Mr. Jason, all my feelings were stirring. I felt sorrow, despair, anger, accomplishment, frustration, love and other feelings I still haven't learned to describe. But I wasn't the only thing that changed. Suddenly there were many more trees in the city than there were two hours ago. The traffic slowed down. The sunset gained majesty. Two days later Mr. Jason was released from the hospital. Four weeks later he died. When I finished my research at the hospital, I made a career change. I left research psychology and began to study counseling.

Psychiatrist Elisabeth Kubler-Ross has found that terminally ill people often come to an acceptance of death before death occurs. Acceptance, however, comes only after struggling through stages of denial, anger, bargaining and depression. The road to the acceptance of death is a rocky one. Once acceptance occurs, however, the person no longer fears or fights death. The individual is one with his destiny:

> It is as if the pain (is) gone, the struggle is over, and there comes a time for the 'final rest before the long journey' as one patient phrased it.[1]

Today most adults have the opportunity to prepare for death. About 90% of adult deaths occur because of fatal diseases such as heart, cancer and stroke. These illnesses progress slowly from onset to termination. Where death used to arrive relatively fast, it now comes slowly.[2] For about 90% of adults, death will become a reality while we live.

Except for the human ostriches who are too afraid to lift their heads and look at life, most of us know that we will not live forever. The fountain of youth is a symbol of creative arrogance. A healthy life style can postpone death, but there is no way to avoid it. Our time on earth is limited. Once we accept this fact, we can begin making mature decisions concerning how we want to spend our time. When we look at the many wonderful things we can do with our lives, time becomes even more rare and valuable than gold, diamonds, rainbows and miracles.

So often we postpone the acceptance of death. In many ways science and technology have aided in this denial. The field of cryogenics is one such dubious advance. Theoretically, a human being with an incurable disease can be frozen until a point in time when a cure is available. To date no such feat has been accomplished, but the growing popularity of the idea is an issue in itself. Some people would rather be frozen indefinitely with the hope of eventually living a little while longer than gracefully and courageously face death. Every time I meet someone who says they would consider cryogenics, I ask them what they would do with the time added to their lives. So far no one has given me a straight answer.

People who deny death are usually unclear on their missions in life. They seem to live with the attitude, "I'll decide later." But as Professor Harold Hill says in *The Music Man*, "If you keep putting everything off till tomorrow, someday you'll turn around and find one big empty yesterday." There are things we need to accomplish today. To-morrow is a gift, not a guarantee.

Another interesting advance which blurs the once clear boundary between life and death is the process of freezing a man's sperm. With this technique, a man can father a child after he dies. A man does not even have to be alive to sire an offspring. So how do we describe this relationship—posthumous parenting?

When we face death we usually feel fear and confusion. If we clear up some of the confusion, we may quell some of the fear. Our technological attempts to defeat death, how-ever, have continued to foster confusion. Expensive machines can keep people alive who, otherwise, would die. To many folks this is a better alternative. But think what it would be like if we conceived of death this way. Imagine if we believed that after we died, our souls would be wheeled into a great big hospital room in the sky. Here we would be hooked up to a machine. We would then spend eternity completely comatose. If this were the case, I doubt anyone could face death much less accept it.

Death is life's most mysterious dimension. No one has ever solved the mystery. We can guess, we can have faith, but we can never know. Without death, humankind might someday run out of questions. Mysteries keep our minds alive. Death stimulates curiosity and adds vitality to life.

Ironically, as mysterious as death is, it provides us with one of life's few bits of certainty. We all die. We have this much certainty in our lives. Life's first rule is that we have only so much time. Life does not last forever. To ignore this rule can result in chaos. We need to recognize our bound-aries and work with what we have. Our limitations can point to a purpose in life. Death suggests that we use our time wisely.

We can live with death as long as its inevitability does not cause us to feel helpless. As long as we are actively involved in the preservation of life, we feel some sense of control. We never have complete control but we need, and can achieve, some control. When a person feels he has no control over his fate, he may become suicidal. Inmates on death row and patients with terminal illnesses frequently attempt suicide. Suicide is a way of regaining control of their fate. Whenever a person feels his fate is completely beyond his control, suicide is a possibility.

We gain a sense of competence and mastery only after we accept the parameters of our existence. We need to know what we have to work with. Then we can arrange priorities. When we come to accept the fact that we have only so much time in life, our priorities usually change. This reordering of priorites begins with the question, "If I had my life to live over, how would I be different?"

Eighty-five year-old Nadine Stair answered the question as follows:

> If I had my life to live over, I'd dare to make more mistakes next time. I'd relax, I'd limber up. I would be sillier than I have been this trip. I would take fewer things seriously. I would take more chances. I would climb more mountains and swim more rivers. I would eat more ice cream and less beans. I would perhaps have more actual troubles, but I'd have fewer imaginary ones.
>
> You see, I'm one of those people who live sensibly and sanely hour after hour, day after day. Oh, I've had my moments, and if I had it to do over again, I'd have more of them. In fact, I'd try to have nothing else. Just moments, one after another, instead of living so many years ahead of each day. I've been one of those persons who never goes anywhere without a thermometer, a

hot water bottle, a raincoat and a parachute. If I had it to do again, I would travel lighter than I have.

If I had my life to live over, I would start barefoot earlier in the spring and stay that way later in the fall. I would go to more dances. I would ride more merry-go-rounds. I would pick more daisies.[3]

Humorist Erma Bombeck addressed the same issue.

If I had my life to live over again, I would have waxed less and listened more.

I would never have insisted the car windows be rolled up on a summer day because my hair had just been teased and sprayed.

I would have invited friends over to dinner even if the carpet was stained and the sofa faded.

I would have eaten popcorn in the 'good' living room and worried less about the dirt when you lit the fireplace.

I would have burned the pink candle sculpted like a rose before it melted while being stored.

I would have sat cross-legged on the lawn with my children and never worried about grass stains.

I would have cried and laughed less while watching television and more while watching real life.

I would have eaten less cottage cheese and more ice cream.

I would have gone to bed when I was sick instead of pretending the earth would go into a holding pattern if I weren't there for a day.

There would have been more I love yous . . . more I'm sorrys . . . more I'm listenings . . . but mostly, given another shot at life, I would seize every minute of it . . .

look at it . . . try it out . . . live it . . . exhaust it . . .
andnever give that minute back until there was nothing
left of it . . .4

Both writers eloquently describe their conceptions of the
happy, healthy life. They would allow for a greater appreciation of life. They feel they have become imprisoned by a
facade of perfection. This facade gets in the way of
happiness.

The question, "If I had my life to live over, what would I
do differently?", is a very therapeutic one. When people
decide what they "would do" differently, they are usually
deciding what they "will do" differently. (Or at least try to do
differently.) We can't change the past. But mistakes made
can improve the present and future.

In counseling sessions I often ask adults what they would
do differently if they could start again from day one. There
seems to be one consistent theme. People say they would try
harder to avoid pretense. They feel they have lost themselves behind their facades. When these adults experience a
secure therapeutic relationship, they come to realize that
they can accept things about themselves which they previously tried to hide. As a person's security increases, he can
accept the unenviable aspects of his being. He can be
himself.

History only records individuality. Posterity only accepts
one's uniqueness. We are remembered for how we were
different from the rest. If we live a life of conformity, we
leave little behind us when we die. This state of affairs
creates an intense fear of death. With no one to remember
us, death means we are not only gone but forgotten. It is as
though we never lived. Here lies man's greatest fear of
death—being forgotten.

We are remembered for our individuality. Or, more precisely, we are remembered for the individuality we express. The more of ourselves we keep bottled up inside, the greater our fear of death. (Even though this fear may be repressed for many years.)

Somewhere inside us all there exists a need to make our lives count for something. How we make an impact on the world is a decision each one of us has to make. We all have the same need, but how we handle this need is an individual matter. The more we feel our lives count for something, the less we fear death. We are not running away from death when we pursue life. Indeed, death encourages a vigorous pursuit of life.

People who run from death usually take shelter in a lifeless world. Hiding in a life without risks, they rarely get involved in life. Being caught between the fear of death and the fear of life can produce a severe psychological crisis. People in this state feel that they must move somewhere but that a move in any direction will be unbearable.

At this point these people must look at what they have tried to deny all along. They must look at life—their lives. They need to understand that their fear is rooted in ignorance. With an adequate support system (i.e. family, friends, counselor) they are better able to look at the difficult questions in life. Support systems must allow for the individual's struggle. People learn from other people that the world does not come to an end when we ask, "What do I want to do to make my life count for something?" or "What can I strive for?" These are healthy questions.

Arrogant people and people with feelings of inferiority are the most likely to avoid life's most difficult dilemmas. The arrogant will not face a question which they cannot easily answer. This would crack their facade of superiority.

People with pervasive feelings of inferiority, on the other hand, feel they are too inadequate to even begin to struggle with questions about the purpose of their lives.

Our self-esteem can keep us from getting involved in life. If we can accept our limitations we will actively explore life. Even though we may not find an ultimate certainty we will learn many things and our lives will have direction. The fact that we may not find all the answers does not make our curiosity useless. Life is not an "all or nothing" proposition. Our limitations should not kill our potential. On the contrary, our limitations should enrich our potential. Just as death can enrich our lives.

The fact that life does not last forever does not detract from its value. I frequently hear depressed clients say, "We all die sooner or later, so what's the point?" This belief, unfortunately, is quite popular in our society. Many people think that life would have more meaning if it lasted forever. I don't know if life would have more meaning, but if life lasted forever no one would be frozen by the fear of death. Maybe things would be better if no one ever died. I don't know.

Since we have to work with our human limitations, however, we need to understand death as a part of our lives. When people wish they wouldn't die it usually means we have more left to do. When we wish that life could last forever we are implying that we could find enough things to keep us happy forever. That says a lot for life.

Now if we compress all that happiness into a finite lifetime, we could have truly wonderful lives. Since we cannot count on forever, we have to act now. Life is too short to be passive. People have more potential than we have time to actualize. The best we can do is the best we can do. Once we accept that we only have so much time, we can begin to live and work with this limitation. Death encourages us to live. We can't wait forever to begin to grow, explore, reach out to others, live. We don't have forever.

Mourning

Mourning is a process of coming to terms with something we cannot do. During this time we struggle to change something we cannot change. When we are faced with the loss of a loved one we do everything we can to deny that reality. Our loved ones are not really gone, we think, until we have tried everything to get them back. Toward this end we wish, demand, pray, swear, scream, cry, reach out, search, deny, hallucinate, beg and then, eventually surrender. We never accept the loss of a loved one because we want to. We come to accept the loss because we have to.

There are those, however, who never psychologically and emotionally accept the loss of their loved ones. Though there are myriad reasons why people hold on to lost relationships, perhaps the majority cannot let go because they cannot grieve. When grief is thought to be an inappropriate show of weakness, it will be repressed.

Unfortunately, western industrial societies have not recognized the human need to fully grieve the loss of a loved one. A week or two after the death all formal ritual (e.g. wake and funeral) is over. Our society's designated period of grief ends abruptly. Except for family and special friends, social support for the bereaved ends with the funeral. This usually means that only within the confines of their homes can the bereaved express their grief.

During the course of grief counseling it is very common to hear bereaved people say, "No one wants to talk about it." Mourning becomes much more difficult when the bereaved cannot share feelings. The widow who finds that no one will listen to her talk about her deceased husband may eventually come to feel ashamed of her feelings. What she needs is someone who has the courage, compassion and patience to listen. Such a friend can help take the shame out of the pain. Pain is an inevitable aspect of grief; shame should not be.

It is critically important that bereaved people be able to share their grief. Grief that refuses expression feeds on itself. It grows like a cancer within the individual. Though the expression of grief may not be encouraged by friends, it is still necessary. When we are in the process of mourning we have a choice. We can grieve publicly for a while or we can grieve privately for the rest of our lives.

Social pressure is not the only thing that inhibits the expression of grief. When we express our hurt, anger, outrage and loneliness, we also express our vulnerability. Mourning is a time of weakness. Besides the mental confusion and the emotional upheaval, there is a greater chance of developing physical illness during the months following an important loss. Healthy mourning requires that we admit to ourselves and to certain people in our lives that we are hurt and that we need support. Bereaved individuals who feel they must remain "the strong one" are likely to have a difficult time. This false bravado represents a refusal to deal with one's grief. Repressed grief, however, swells within. Sooner or later it must be dealt with.

In short, problems arise when we are ashamed to grieve. The loss of a loved one requires a tremendous psychological adaptation. A person's world changes radically with the loss of a loved one. Mourning is the process where people adjust to their new world. No mourning—no adjustment.

After the death of a loved one the first discovery people make is that life is not fair. Good people die while bad people survive. Children die. Murders go unsolved. The structure which "fairness" gave to life is now gone. The bereaved wonders if there are any rules to live by.

Death, especially a sudden death, leaves us with an intense feeling of how unpredictable life is. Security vanishes for a time and may never be restored completely. The bereaved person's world is without structure. During bereavement people often feel they are losing their minds. They feel weak and vulnerable in an unfriendly world. This is complicated by the fact that family and friends may not want to talk about the death. Mourning can leave a person feeling very isolated.

The bereaved person suffers. Deep inside most of us realize this. So why is it so hard for most of us to talk with and comfort the bereaved? Dr. Beverly Raphael believes that our own fear of death can keep us from trying to understand and support a bereaved friend. ". . . empathy with the bereaved in their encounters with loss and death touches off in each one of us the most personal of terrors."[5] When we see someone mourning, we witness our own worst nightmare. We each fight to avoid the conclusion that since loss occurs to people, it can happen to me.

The loneliness which is so common during bereavement stems from more than the loss of the loved one. Many people avoid friends in mourning. The bereaved often feels cut off from the community. Because we have such a difficult time facing the bereaved, most people have very little understanding of grief.

A popular conception of grief is that it is a sad time. Grief is seen as similar to sorrow, depression or despair. Though this is certainly true, there is so much more to grief. Grief also contains anger. In many people, in fact, the intensity of anger surpasses that of sorrow. This is especially true in the early phases of mourning.

Anger fuels the fight to reclaim the lost loved one. The bereaved individual feels he can accomplish this mission if he tries hard enough. The bereaved do not give up without a fight. Humans have a healthy tendency to test reality. Before letting go we try many things.

The bereaved may also feel anger toward their departed loved one. They frequently feel deserted, as if the deceased willfully decided to leave them. The bereaved may scream at the deceased for leaving or they may swear at God for taking their loved one. Early in the grieving process emotions such as anger contain more power than rational thought. All rational thinking can do is remind the bereaved that the loss is irreversible. Emotions seek to silence this voice of reality.

The death of a loved one is perhaps the most humbling experience people can know in life. Devoting one's entire being to the retrieval of the deceased leaves one with a total sense of helplessness. This is the feeling, "I've never wanted anything so bad yet come up so empty." The person who has never been able to accept human limitations will have a very difficult time with bereavement. Bereavement is a time of recognizing the limitations of humankind. It also involves the ordeal of accepting these limitations.

People can postpone and deny their bereavement. In the short run this may contain the pain. But the loss must eventually be grieved. If a person cannot grieve it is unlikely that he will be able to return to a healthy state of being. It is crucial that the bereaved develop the humility to accept the things they cannot change.

In the early stages of grief, the bereaved must come to accept two things in order to work through their anger. The bereaved must first accept that the deceased cannot return and, second, that the deceased did not choose to leave. In both cases the bereaved acknowledges that people cannot control death.

The widow, for example, must eventually accept that her husband will no longer walk through the front door. He will never again call to say he will be late for dinner. For a time it will be impossible for her to accept this. Her inability to retrieve her husband results in a deep sense of helplessness. Only with the passage of time and the support of family and friends can this widow come to recognize and accept that her helplessness is a part of the human condition. This acceptance does not make her situation pleasant, but it will put an end to the frustration and depression which comes with trying to raise the dead.

In order to assuage her anger she must come to the realization that, just as she cannot resuscitate her dead husband, he cannot decide to return to her. Leaving her was not his idea. (Except, of course, in the case of suicide.) He was as helpless in the face of death as she is now. And that is because they are human beings. The pain of grief is inescapable. In order to help someone resolve grief, we need to see that they work through the shame and the blame. Healthy people grieve their losses. They also, eventually, realize that no one is to blame.

People have a much greater chance of resolving grief if we feel supported by others. We have an easier time dropping defenses and facades if we live in an environment where we feel safe. Since so many people avoid discussing death, it may be difficult to find sufficient support. In order to feel supported in our grief we need people who care for us and accept us while we are hurt, scared and a little bit crazy.

Support groups for the bereaved are developing all over the country. These organizations provide a tremendous service to grief stricken families. Their grief no longer isolates them from other people. In these groups the bereaved become part of a community which allows them to express their grief. This kind of support takes the shame out of the pain. It is easier to express oneself when one feels understood and accepted.

Support groups for the bereaved also help those who have worked through their grief. These people can find meaning in their own suffering by using their experience to help others. One who has experienced the pain of grief can empathize with the struggles of the newly bereaved. The bereaved can do things for each other that mental health professionals cannot do for them. They know where the other has been.

The individual who survives grief has a lot to contribute to the community as long as he can draw from his experience. Many people try to forget their bereavement. They view this time as a tragedy which could not possibly contribute anything positive to life. The experience is banished from consciousness. They avoid thoughts of bereavement. They also avoid people who are suffering the loss of a loved one.

The courageous being who seeks to learn from every experience can find valuable lessons in grief. People can learn, albeit the hard way, how much relationships mean. We learn how much people need people—how much we need others and how much others need us. The bereaved can come to a deeper understanding of the human condition. They may develop a deep sense of humility. The confrontation with death can be a very humbling experience. The bereaved learns how much they can love and how much they can lose.

Support groups are based on humility. In order to become part of these groups people need to openly admit two things: 1) "I have a problem" and 2) "I need people to help me." The facade of total self-sufficiency must be checked at the door. An attitude of arrogance, which denies the need for help, only serves to increase the distance between people. Bereaved people often wear this facade to protect themselves from more pain. Several days after the death of her husband, a seventy-five year-old widow said to me, "It makes you wonder if it's worth getting that close to someone." The bereaved are often torn between the wish to protect themselves and the need for other people. And they know better than anyone how much people need people.

It takes humility to ask for help, to reach out to others. It also takes humility for the bereaved to survive on their own. Being alone can highlight one's limitations especially if the loved one compensated for certain flaws. A widow may not have the strength to do repairs around the house. A widower may not have his wife's education and consequently have more difficulty helping his children with their homework. People sometimes enter relationships in order to compensate for what they cannot do. When the relationship ends they are reminded of their shortcomings.

There are many reasons why mourning is such a difficult process. Friends and relatives who wish to help the bereaved can do so by allowing them to experience and express their grief. This means communicating the message, "I know grief can be very painful. You need to do what you have to to get through this difficult time. I will do my best to leave you alone when you need to be left alone. I will also do my best to stand by you and support you while you scream and cry and talk and talk and talk."

A friend cannot erase the pain of bereavement. A friend can, however, help the bereaved gradually work through this difficult time.

Conclusion

Death is quite a paradox. It remains life's greatest mystery, and yet it provides us with a sense of certainty. We don't know what death is, but it happens to all of us. If we choose to face this limitation, we can develop a clearer understanding of life. We don't have forever.

Denying death means taking life for granted. Though this may provide some security, it also creates boredom. Without an awareness of death, people tend to procrastinate. It's easy to put off till tomorrow if there is an endless supply of tomorrows.

The death of a loved one puts an abrupt halt to the denial of death. During the mourning process we struggle to accept the conditions of life. We learn how painful life can be. We learn how precious life is. Sometimes bereaved people feel guilt for ever having taken life for granted. Some folks find the courage to keep growing. Others wither and die.

Death can kill us. Or death can encourage us to live.

CHAPTER SIX

On Being Different

"There are so many things I can't do already."
— David — a disabled 18 year-old
who recently learned that he may soon
lose feeling in the right side of his face.

Everyone dies. Accepting our mortality does not isolate us. Indeed it gives us something in common with all other forms of life. Life's ultimate limitation may terrify us at times, but it does not make us inferior to anyone else. We do not hear people say they are ashamed of themselves because they will someday die. Nor do we hear people say they are ashamed of anyone else for dying.

Death represents life's ultimate limitation. We all face this boundary. Facing death involves conquering fear and anxiety. Death may scare us but it does not humiliate anyone. Our mortality does not make us weaker than others or less than human.

There are limitations, however, which cause certain people to feel they are less than human. Handicapped people, obese people and ugly people are all aware, on some level, that they are different. It may sound cruel to identify any individual or group of individuals as ugly. I do so because there is a sizable portion of the population who consider their appearance to be completely unacceptable. There is also a large number of people who discriminate against other men and women who do not meet personal standards of attractiveness. The obese and the ugly are denied social opportunities.

In this chapter, I use the term "disabled" to describe the obese, the ugly and all people our culture typically describes as handicapped. The disabled are especially susceptible to developing feelings of inadequacy. They are most likely to consider themselves "have nots" and "can't dos." A single physical disability can lead to a pervasive feeling of shame.

The disabled person is not disabled in all areas of his being, at least not at first. Obesity, for example, is a physical condition and not a character flaw. The disabled are most likely to be discriminated against by people who see a handicap as a state of being. In this case, the paraplegic person is treated as though he had mental and spiritual limitations just as severe as his physical problem. If the disabled person encounters this attitude in the majority of his relationships, he may come to see himself this way.

Being different from the rest can lead to feelings of being isolated or separated from the rest. As I discussed previously, low self-esteem leads to withdrawal from other people which, in turn, leads to lower self-esteem. Without the proper help, the situation continues to deteriorate.

At one point or another everyone feels low in self-esteem. Life frequently presents circumstances which remind us that we are not as capable as we would like to be. Hopefully, however, our bouts with low self-esteem are brief. They serve as helpful reminders of our need for humility. Sometimes we are not as competent as we would like to be.

When low self-esteem remains, serious problems can arise. Chronic and severe low self-esteem results in shame. The person who feels ashamed of himself will continue to shy away from people. He will feel inferior by comparison and consequently vulnerable to ridicule. The separation from other human beings leads to feelings of social inadequacy which, in turn, lowers self-esteem. It is virtually impossible to bolster one's self-esteem while isolated from other people.

People who are ashamed of themselves sometimes seek friendships with other "losers." Low self-esteem teenagers, for example, look for companionship in the drug and delinquent subcultures. This is where they feel they belong. But here again, this context is not conducive to building a healthy self-concept.

At this point, I need to clarify the distinction between guilt and shame. These two terms are frequently confused and hence hinder the expression of one's feelings. If I feel guilt, I feel remorse for WHAT I HAVE DONE. I feel guilt for having committed a crime or a sin or for violating certain ethical standards. Guilt is the result of a specific thought or action.

If I feel shame, I feel remorse for WHO I AM. I am ashamed of myself if I feel inadequate, or worse, unlovable. As I have mentioned, people can accept many unenviable aspects of their lives. We cannot, however, accept ourselves if we believe we are unlovable. The feeling of being unlovable defies humility. We can never accept this state of being.

There are different degrees of shame. Even in its mildest form, however, it can make life miserable. In its early stages, shame is a feeling of general inadequacy and unacceptability. The person believes he is incapable of creating a good life. He may feel incapable of creating anything worthwhile. Shame also suggests a comparison with others. The individual believes he does not measure up to the people with whom he compares himself.

In the early stages of shame, the individual maintains a faint hope that somehow, someday things may turn around. If he actively pursues this goal, his prognosis improves. Working to attain competency in the tasks of life greatly increases one's chances of eliminating shame. Things happen when people make them happen.

Severe problems arise, however, when shameful people passively wait for their situation to change. Such people often fall into the Lottery Syndrome (see Chapter III). They sit and wait for fairy godmothers. They think the only things that can save them are magic and miracles. But shame cannot be exorcised by a passive approach. Passivity, in this case, spawns feelings of ineffectiveness. For every person who wins the lottery, there are millions who do not.

Shame is usually thought to result from a lack of confidence. To an extent, this is true. But shame also stems from the absence of humility. We all have crosses to bear. Maybe you can't paint a masterpiece or drive in the Indianapolis 500 or write beautiful music. Maybe you can't climb Mount Everest or cure cancer or understand opera. Maybe you can't see or hear or speak or manage in the bathroom by yourself. We become ashamed of ourselves when we do not accept the limitations which we cannot change. Until we accept the defects which we cannot improve, we will experience feelings of shame. The healthy individual, whether he be disabled or "normal," feels proud for what he can do and humble for what he cannot.

Those who do not develop the humility to accept their limitations gradually fall deeper and deeper into shame. As the feeling of shame becomes more pervasive, the individual will continue to distance himself from other people. The situation is now bad and getting worse. Without the support of a warm human relationship, the person will eventually come to feel unlovable. The best thing we can call this situation is "hitting the bottom."

Once a person comes to feel he is unlovable, he gives up on humanity. His preferred mode of behavior is violence. He may be suicidal or he may direct his anger toward others. Humankind has yet to find an adequate way to deal with people once they have reached this stage. The most intelligent approaches, however, have aimed at prevention. How do we do this? There is a bumper sticker which answers this best, "For every child a hand to hold."

There is one final point about shame which deserves attention. Shame so often goes unrecognized. People are much more willing to admit to feeling guilty. In counseling, clients frequently say things like, "I always feel guilty" or "It seems as though I'm always doing the wrong thing." When people report chronic feelings of guilt, I usually find—when I look a little deeper—that their real problem concerns shame. People will forever feel they are doing (or have done) the wrong thing, if they feel they are not capable of doing the right thing. A person who is ashamed of himself feels incapable of doing the right thing.

Helping people in this condition means dealing with the real issue. During counseling, I do not get caught up in an argument about whether they were right or wrong in specific situations. Rather, I focus on their self-concept. I want to help them identify what keeps them from feeling competent. Then I want to support them and encourage them to remove that obstacle.

Shame is a special problem for disabled people. By definition, they have more to be ashamed about. They are "the unfortunates." Approximately 40 million Americans have physical or mental disabilities.[1] If we add the people who are denied certain privileges because of their physical appearance, we begin to realize how many people are conspicuously flawed.

People with conspicuous flaws acquire shame the same way everyone else does. Acceptance by others precedes the acceptance of self. If one grows up feeling rejected by others, he is likely to eventually reject himself. If he rejects himself, he is likely to reject others. The crisis is contagious.

Disabled people are more likely to develop feelings of shame, but NOT because of their disabilities per se. Disabled people are more likely to develop shame because they are more likely to be rejected by others. "Prejudicial attitudes toward disabled persons often constitute a greater barrier to successful adjustment than does the actual disabling condition."[2]

Attitudes Toward the Disabled

Disability is not a state of being. At least not at first. Disability describes a relationship. Without the concept "normal," there would be no concept "disabled." The disabled person's disabilities become apparent only when seen in relationship with non-disabled people. In the same manner, the limitations of human beings become obvious when we compare ourselves to other forms of life. If birds are normal, for instance, then we are disabled because we cannot fly.

Disabled people are constantly reminded that they are different. Depending on the severity of their condition, they may need the help of a live-in caretaker. This caretaker serves as a reminder of what they cannot do for themselves. The fact that they are different is clear and yet "different" is not, in itself, cause for shame.

A person, disabled or non-disabled, will develop shame if he feels he is rejected for his individuality. Due to our cultural biases, the disabled are at risk of developing these feelings. Research indicates that disabled persons often live with unfavorable attitudes from a very early age because even their parents have difficulty treating them normally.[3] We also know that disabled children are more likely to be abused.[4]

In the community, things are not much better. People who lack the "look of success" are routinely discriminated against. Disabled people see their reflections in eyes that say, "There but for the grace of God go I." Non-disabled people tend to think they are the only ones blessed with the graces of God.

The most popular form of discrimination against the disabled is avoidance. The non-disabled, for the most part, distance themselves from the disabled. This represents the old "out of sight, out of mind" principle. Philip Slater described this situation:

> Our ideas about institutionalizing the aged, psychotic, retarded and infirm are based on a pattern of thought that we might call The Toilet Assumption—the notion that unwanted matter, unwanted difficulties, unwanted complexities and obstacles will disappear if they are removed from our immediate field of vision. . . . Our approach to social problems is to decrease their visibility; out of sight, out of mind. . . .[5]

Though there are probably many reasons why the disabled remain ignored, I will focus on two possibilities. First, the disabled serve as reminders of human fallibility. The disabled remind the non-disabled that certain limitations cannot be overcome. Second, the non-disabled have their egos massaged by clearly differentiating themselves from the disabled. If I am not "disabled," then I must be "abled" (i.e. free from serious flaws). It is as though the disabled and the non-disabled are two different forms of life.

The most insidious form of self-esteem is that which is based on the pain of others. In this case, a person is satisfied knowing that others are worse off. He can then breathe a sigh of relief that he does not exist at the bottom of the pile. In order to stay off the bottom, however, he must do what he can to keep others down. Some folks even have the nerve to call this the "American way" in an attempt to justify their bigotry. This is merely an ignorant attempt to give their cruelty a cause.

Bigotry represents an attempt to praise one's self without accepting one's self. It is a way of being "better" without necessarily being "good." The majority of bigots have little self-esteem.

The non-disabled individual who recognizes and accepts his flaws will be capable of relating well with a disabled person. Research indicates that people with positive and secure self-concepts tend to show more positive and accepting attitudes toward those with disabilities, while people with low self-concepts often reject them. People who are more secure and confident in their own selves, tend to feel more positive and accepting of people with disabilities.[6]

The individual who is willing to accept his own flaws, can recognize that *we are all disabled to some extent*. Disabled people and non-disabled people have more similarities than differences. We share the privilege called life. We share the feelings which come with being human. We share the need for each other.

Non-disabled people and disabled people differ in degree rather than kind. The non-disabled enjoy certain freedoms which the disabled do not. And, very often, vice versa. But we all know restrictions. No one can fly, live forever, or live happily with the feeling that one is unlovable.

Efforts to avoid disabled people represents an attempt to run away from one's own shortcomings. The person who cannot adjust to an imperfect world cannot adjust to life. The challenge of life is the challenge to work within our limitations. Consequently, people with disabilities are sometimes called "People with special challenges." But their challenges may differ from those of the non-disabled only in that the challenges of disabled people are more obvious. We might think of people with disabilities as "people who cannot hide their limitations." Or, in some cases, "people who choose not to hide themselves and their limitations."

Hidden Disabilities

Much to the chagrin of the bigots, not all disabilities are readily apparent. Certain sizable physical limitations, through the help of make-up, clothing or prostheses, never catch the public eye. In spite of this, the person may still feel different. The potential for feelings of inferiority exists. This inferiority grows if the person feels isolated. If the mastectomy patient feels her "secret" creates a distance between her and the people she cares for, her prognosis worsens. Sometimes the secret can get in the way of support.

There is nothing wrong or unhealthy about covering up a flaw. Everyone is entitled to their privacy. I see no reason why we should expose ourselves for all to see. At the same time, however, people do not do well psychologically when we feel we must hide ourselves. This apparent contradiction has a simple solution.

People need to be understood and accepted by certain other people—*not the whole world*. When we enter intimate relationships, we are deciding who we will allow to know us. There is a risk, but the risk is a necessary one. There can be no emotional health or happiness without risk. We hope the people we open up to can understand and then accept. The feeling of being understood and accepted is very similar to the feeling of being loved.

Because human beings have feelings, we can be hurt. Expressing our limitations leaves us vulnerable to rejection and to "the whole world finding out." Yet we feel the need to take this risk. The alternative would be to keep important aspects of our being hidden away. Keeping significant dimensions of ourselves locked inside leads to loneliness. Loneliness describes the feeling that no one really knows me.

We keep such secrets if we feel that other people would not accept us if they *really* knew us. When we reach this conclusion, the secrets stay in and the facades go up. Facades are O.K. (i.e. normal) as long as they can come down to allow for close interpersonal relationships. Facades protect us from bigots, but not everyone is a bigot. There is a human need to reveal ourselves. The people we reveal ourselves to are called friends and loved ones.

Deep inside, we all need to know how acceptable we are to others. We can accept ourselves as we are only after we have experienced at least one relationship where we are accepted for being ourselves. We are not acceptable to ourselves until we have experienced understanding and acceptance from others. Hopefully, such a relationship exists between the parent and the child. Sometimes this relationship comes much later in life. Sometimes it never happens.

People who can look back on relationships where they were genuinely accepted have an important advantage in life. They know firsthand that they are lovable. If later in life, through illness or injury, a person develops certain defects or disabilities, he may begin to ask, "Am I still lovable?" He may feel that the person he was, no longer exists.

If I change "who I am," I will need to know if the new me is acceptable to anyone. There is only one way to find out. The new me needs to expose myself to a friend or a loved one. The answer will follow.

People desire to be understood by others. This desire will be repressed, however, if we believe that exposing ourselves will be too painful. When relationships are too painful to continue, there is no adequate shelter. Withdrawing into ourselves also produces pain. The only solution is to choose friends carefully and then take the risks that come with revealing ourselves.

Disability as a State of Being

I stated previously that "disability" describes a particular type of interpersonal relationship. The person with a disability lacks certain freedoms which come with being abled. Because of their obvious defects, the disabled are frequently treated as different. Like everyone else, how the disabled are treated by others affects how the person sees himself and feels about himself.

When people with disabilities are constantly treated as "disabled" rather than as "people," feelings of inferiority are likely to develop. When someone lives with the stigma of being different, he probably knows the feeling of being isolated. "Different" creates a distance between people. To be a little different—or to be very different in certain areas (i.e. special talents)—creates a healthy distance which allows for individuality. To be really different (i.e. disabled) can result in an unhealthy distance. The pattern soon emerges: isolation ▶ low self-esteem ▶ more isolation ▶ lower self-esteem ▶ and so on and so on.

It is easy for disabled people to internalize the reactions of others. It is hard not to. A person with a facial disfigurement, for example, learns something by watching others try not to look at him. He learns that he makes some people uncomfortable. Obese people live with the prejudice that equates fat with lazy. The disabled are those of us who have an especially difficult time being accepted for who we are. It seems that so many people would prefer to pursue a friendship with someone who is pretty and healthy.

When a person internalizes the self-concept called "disabled," he will begin to cooperate with the bigots. He will voluntarily present himself as inferior. Eye contact will decrease, shoulders will slump and hopes for happy endings will fade. Just as his world cannot accept him, he can no longer accept himself. Values become confused. The individual now thinks of humility as the attempt to accept himself as a total failure. Seeing oneself as a failure, however, suggests that the person cannot accept anything about himself.

When the feeling of being disabled reaches the core of an individual, the real problem is no longer primarily physical. The most serious aspect of the disability is now psychological. A personal history filled with rejection and discrimination cannot be erased with surgery. The removal of physical disabilities does not necessarily lead to improved psychological adjustment.[7] When feelings of weakness and inferiority pervade one's being, the emotional pain can last a lifetime.

Of course, not all disabled people wind up with feelings of inferiority. Given the attitudes of our society, it's a wonder more don't. It seems that an accepting friend or family can counter some of the adverse reactions to an unaccepting society. People don't need to be accepted by everyone if we know we are, or have been, loved by someone.

If disabled people internalize the attitudes of an unaccepting society, the prognosis is poor. Efforts to be understood and accepted will cease. This is the foundation of so much chronic mental illness.

So we come to the question, "How can a disabled person develop a healthy self-concept while faced with so much discrimination?" The answer is this: a single loving relationship can counter the effects of many rejections. Quality beats the hell out of quantity. A person can be happy living with "a face only a mother could love" as long as there is someone who loves that face. People don't need to look like movie stars or move like professional athletes in order to find happiness. But we do need to know we are capable of being loved.

Conclusion

Not too long ago I spent a snowy afternoon stranded in a large metropolitan airport. After an hour or so of looking at magazine covers, riding escalators and marking time, I sat down to do some serious people watching. I wasn't there long when I saw a little girl sitting under a chair. She was about four or five years old. Before I knew it, we were helping each other reduce the boredom.

She didn't speak much but kept a big smile. I asked her questions which she answered with a nod, a shake of her head or a shrug of her shoulders. She was a pretty child with long blonde hair, big eyes and a beautiful smile. I remember thinking how happy she seemed.

Before long the little girl's activity began to increase. She began to do some spins. As she spun around, I saw two large hearing aids. I immediately felt surprised and a little uncertain. Her mother then came over to settle her down. The mother grabbed the little girl's shoulders, looked her straight in the face and told her gently, yet firmly, to stop.

The mother and I then began to converse. She told me that her daughter was deaf but that she was enrolled in a wonderful school for "total communication." At this school the children learn both sign language and lip reading. I remarked to the mother how, until I saw the hearing aids, I didn't suspect any kind of problem. It certainly seemed as though the school for total communication had done a marvelous job.

The mother agreed that her daughter had developed many important communication skills. But just as the long blonde hair covered the hearing aids, the girl had developed ways of disguising other aspects of her disability. Most notably, if her daughter did not understand a message, she would not ask for that message to be repeated. She would never say "What?". She usually changed the subject, created a distraction or pretended she was too shy to respond. She wouldn't let on.

Later, as I boarded my plane, I thought of a friend of mine. This friend also has a hearing impairment. I searched my memory for an instance when my middle-aged friend asked for a message to be repeated. Though he often leaves his hearing aid at home, I couldn't remember him ever saying "What?".

Most children enjoy asking for a message to be repeated. They find the added attention enjoyable. When they say "I didn't hear," it doesn't mean "I can't hear." Children with healthy ears are not exposing themselves when they admit they missed something. But the kids who need to ask the most, find it the hardest. Asking "What?" means admitting a defect.

The little girl in the airport had so much to be proud of. I still find it amazing that such young children can learn to lip read and use sign language. Her school deserves a lot of credit for teaching her ways to handle her disability. I wonder if they help the children learn to accept themselves?

As I discussed in chapter three, it is almost impossible for children to learn humility. Children tenaciously hold on to their belief in magic. They cannot understand why anyone would accept a painful situation as permanent when the situation will change someday by magic.

So how do disabled people acquire the humility to accept permanent limitations? How do disabled people come to accept both the physical limitations and the reactions of bigots? What keeps a hearing impaired adult from saying, "I'm sorry, I didn't hear you"?

Before anyone can accept oneself, one needs to experience being accepted by someone else. If someone feels unacceptable to others because of a particular flaw, that flaw will be hidden (if at all possible). If, on the other hand, the individual feels he can share his disability and maintain a secure, accepting relationship, he will probably feel free to ask for assistance.

Children fear isolation more than anything else. They become anxious and then depressed if they feel left out or left behind. Contrary to popular belief, adults never outgrow this fear. Though many courageous adults risk separation for the sake of a value or cause, the isolation remains a painful price to pay.

Admitting a limitation is itself a cause. The disabled person can say, "I shouldn't be made to feel ashamed." No one is perfect, yet no one need be ashamed. Shame is a lie. Everyone has something to offer. Everyone is potentially "good enough." In addition, we are all, in some way, disabled.

When I demand that I be perfect, I become ashamed that I am not. A compulsive desire for perfection does not lead to perfection. It leads to shame.

CHAPTER SEVEN

No Humility, No Stability

*Humility is just as much the opposite of
self-abasement as it is of self-exaltation.*
— Dag Hammarskjold

A biologist once told me, "When you come across those times in life when you feel like garbage, just remember that at the moment you were conceived, out of all the sperms which were fighting for the job, you were the fastest and the strongest."

The fact that we have life should be a source of pride. Surviving the past represents a tremendous accomplishment. The future, on the other hand, waits for our potential. And we have more potential than we have time to actualize. Inherent in life there are so many things to be proud of.

As wonderful as life can be, we have the ability to imagine it being even better. We can imagine life without a single flaw, shortcoming, defect, limitation or problem. If we live in this dream, we never come to know ourselves or our world. We begin to explore life when we can face the unpleasantries as well as the accomplishments. When we accept that life consists of good and not-so-good, we can really start learning from life.

The healthiest personalities can accept themselves and their friends and loved ones for who they are. These individuals do not feel the need to change everything in their lives in order to find contentment. They can accept that some things will remain as they are.

The hardest thing to accept about life is the pain. Pain comes in the form of sickness, injury, disappointment and frustration. Emotional pain is rooted in our inability to do things we would like to do. We experience emotional anguish when our lives fall short of what we imagine they should be.

When we feel that life is not as it should be, we have two options. We can work to change ourselves and move toward the life we dream of. In order to accomplish this task, we need healthy feelings of pride. Our second option requires that we reevaluate the lives we pursue. These ideal lives may require changes which we are not capable of making. Sometimes we have to forego the ideal and accept the real. In order to accomplish this task, we need healthy feelings of humility.

Pride and humility give each other meaning and nobility. Without humility, pride swells to arrogance. Without pride, humility fades into passivity and inferiority. One cannot have too much pride if there exists an equal supply of humility (and vice versa). In healthy individuals, humility and pride grow together.

To gain an accurate understanding of ourselves, we must consider both our strengths and our weaknesses. If we only face the positive dimensions of our being, a large portion of ourselves remains in the dark. The same holds true for people who only face their limitations. They only know part of themselves.

Not knowing what you can and cannot do is like living with a strange, large animal. You wouldn't feel comfortable with it until you knew something about this animal. Is it friendly? Is it cruel and sadistic? Does it fly? Can I kill it? Is it smart, stupid or both? What makes it angry? Does it have friends? Do I want to be friends with it? Should I ignore it? Can I trust it? Is it wild or tame? Will it hurt me?

Now let's say you were stuck on a very small island with this animal—an island so small that you could not get out of each other's sight. You could run from the animal but never really get away from it. What would you do?

It's sad to see someone being chased by the strange, large animal. Such people are always on the move. As the animal chases them, it becomes larger and more ferocious. When the animal catches them (which is inevitable), their movement stops. Then they act as if they were trapped within the intestines of the beast. These people feel overwhelmed by life.

So many of us live as though we had strange, large animals pursuing us. The animals symbolize the aspects of ourselves which we perceive as repulsive and frightening. These dimensions remain strange and animal-like until we try to understand them. Once we make an effort to understand our "dark side," the lights start to come on. The strange animal becomes more familiar, less scary and more human.

An accurate appraisal of ourselves requires that we face the positive and the not-so-positive dimensions of our lives. We get stuck and stop growing when there are not enough things to explore. Though we may feel bored, life is never boring. Sometimes we are too afraid of what we might find to release our curiosities.

We develop stable yet growing personalities when we learn to accept ourselves and our worlds. This does not mean we should try to stay the same. On the contrary, when we have an understanding of ourselves, we can plot the direction of our growth. With an understanding of ourselves, we can honestly answer such questions as, "What do I need?" and "Who do I need?"

The less we know about ourselves, the darker our worlds (inner and outer) become. We trip over things and run into walls. To keep others from looking inside us, we can construct facades. The thicker a person's facade, the greater his shame. He feels incapable of honestly expressing himself.

Facades tend to vary depending on the audience. A facade is constructed for the sake of gaining acceptance. Because different audiences desire different qualities, the individual who is addicted to social acceptance must accommodate these whims. The facade-shrouded person must change complexions like a chameleon.

Those who have the courage and humility to express themselves with all their shortcomings live with greater freedom and consistency. They can say, "This is the real me, corns and all!" These people change because they love to grow and not because they feel their real self is unacceptable.

So how do we come to know ourselves? Well, because we change, the process of learning about ourselves is continuous. We can never know ourselves once and for all. Both the questions and the answers change. We can, however, know ourselves in the here and now. We come to understand ourselves through the examination of our experiences. If we accept and integrate the good and the bad, we will maintain healthy and stable personalities.

This book has focused on the importance of facing and accepting the painful aspects of our being. I call these painful aspects our limitations. The limitations which cannot be changed can either be accepted or denied. Limitations, however, feed on denial. In the dark they fester and swell.

Accepting our limitations means accepting ourselves as imperfect. We all have limitations to deal with. In the words of renowned educator Dr. Leo Buscaglia, "The wise are just as capable of being confused as the retarded."[1] Expressing our imperfection is perhaps the clearest expression of our humanness. Admitting our needs and limitations proves that we are indeed genuine human beings.

When we attempt more than we can accomplish, we encounter failure. Failure represents the potential consequence of ambition. The fear of failure can destroy ambition. Learning to accept failure reduces the risks involved in trying. This does not mean that one should learn to like failure. You do not have to like an experience in order to accept it or learn from it.

Maybe we all should take a course on failure.[2] In such a course we could learn ways to cope with failure, maybe even how to learn from failure. A failure can be a very powerful learning and humbling experience. The love of learning can help us face failure. If our educational institutions expect to promote lifelong learning, they need to sensitize individuals to those aspects of life which are rich in information. Failure is one such area.

The only environments which completely squelch growth are those which cannot teach us anything. I know of no such circumstances. Certainly there are contexts which are more conducive to learning and growth than others. But we have the potential to learn wherever we are. Consider the wisdom of Viktor Frankl and Elie Wiesel who survived, and dare I say matured, through their experiences in German concentration camps. We can learn anywhere.

We can learn from our suffering. I do not mean to imply, however, that learning erases all pain and misery. The experience of pain, both physical and emotional, seems inherent in the human condition. But our pain need not be a useless experience. Lessons learned from this condition can improve our lives. To maximize our potential, we must minimize our useless experiences. We can do this by learning from all our experiences.

I am a firm believer that we should all, at some time in our lives, be the victims of an injustice. This is a tremendously important experience. Having our rights denied or our dignity ignored can ignite one's sense of purpose. This sense of purpose serves as the remedy for apathy. A slap in the face can really wake us up.

Though we experience suffering in our lives, all our experiences are valuable. We can waste an experience by not learning from it, but no experience is, in itself, useless. Every experience has a lesson.

Too often we come away from an unpleasant experience with a very narrow understanding of the event. This understanding only addresses how we may avoid a recurrence. We tend to see failures, mistakes and humiliations as forms of punishment. We learn as children that all we need to know about punishment is how to avoid it. This is unfortunate because growth can be painful. If we avoid the pain, we may avoid the gain.

The basis of laziness as well as many forms of mental illness is a person's refusal to face difficult experiences—past, present and future. Difficult tasks become impossible tasks for the individual who can neither ask for help nor learn from hard times. This individual remains alone and ignorant.

We would all like to believe that nothing is impossible, but this is just not so. We cannot rid life of its unpleasantries. In order to face, accept and learn from our limitations we must develop a mature sense of humility. Humility allows us to adjust and grow and learn in spite of our imperfection.

Humility also serves as a constant reminder that, just like everyone else, we have flaws.

We grow when we accept the fact that certain areas of our being will never change. These permanent aspects of our lives are frequently very difficult to accept. But there are rewards. Carl Rogers summarized this better than I when he wrote, "It becomes easier for me to accept myself as a decidedly imperfect person, who by no means functions at all times in the way in which I would like to perform. . . . the curious paradox is that when I accept myself as I am, then I change."[3] The change Rogers speaks of is positive change or growth. We grow when we accept the aspects of ourselves which can grow no further.

Daring to admit a flaw may even correct that problem. As I look back over my own history, I cringe when I think of all the questions I did not ask because I was afraid I would sound stupid. If I would have admitted my ignorance, I would be wiser today. But I guess I learned from my folly. I ask a lot of questions these days. (And yes, I do occasionally sound stupid . . . but life goes on.)

I began chapter one by defining humility as the acceptance of one's own imperfections. Humility does not restrict self-expression nor does it disallow feelings of pride. Humility in no way limits human potential. Rather humility allows us to accept the limitations of our potential.

The more we can accept of ourselves, the more we can express. Humility allows us to express who we really are. We cannot be perfect and we do not have to be. We can be proud of ourselves as imperfect human beings.

Humility is an art, a feeling, a value, a virtue, a human quality, an education, and other things which I am not clever enough to think of. But humility is not everything. Humility cannot replace love, courage, wisdom, patience, trust, honesty or any other value. Humility is no more important than any other value. But it is just as important as any other value. Humility is one of several crucial ingredients in emotional health and happiness.

Unlike other values, however, humility has never received much respect or attention. There are very few songs, metaphors or legends designed to give one an understanding or a feel for humility. I like to think that somewhere deep in a cave or beneath some ancient ruins or in the darkest corner of an undiscovered castle there sits a wonderful collection of art and literary works which were designed to educate humanity on the art of humility. Maybe we'll find it someday. I wonder if anyone would care?

And if we found such a collection, I wonder what it would say? I wonder what is the best way to teach humility?

I don't have the answers, but I do have some thoughts. We cannot learn humility until we want to learn humility. And if we want to learn, then we have found humility. We feel the need to know when we realize that we do not know. We ask questions when we can accept that we do not know. We feel proud when we learn. We feel humble when we find new questions.

We grow close to other people as we allow ourselves to need them. Perhaps the greatest gift two people can give each other is their vulnerability. We afford our friends and loved ones the utmost respect when we accept their imperfection. In this way we welcome them to the human race. Two people who help each other grow always grow together.

We live in a universe we did not create. We owe our lives to a Higher Power who we do not have the intelligence to completely understand. We did not wish or will our own births. We cannot take credit for the potential we were born with. We live in the midst of a shared uncertainty. And though life's uncertainties can be terrifying, we have the potential to accept our lives. We also have the potential to accept each other.

We come to a most crucial question, "How can we find security in a world we cannot control?" The arrogant person, of course, will attempt to deny anything he cannot control. He becomes king of a very small planet.

Only the humble person can comprehend the complexity of our universe. This is not to say that a humble person understands everything that goes on in the universe. Rather, humility keeps our egos from getting in the way of our senses. A humble person can see and hear and feel more clearly.

A humble person can appreciate the depth of life because this person does not crumble as his context expands. Only inflated egos can be deflated. Those based in reality can perceive reality.

But reality can be terrifying. Erich Fromm once wrote, "Free man is by necessity insecure; thinking man is by necessity uncertain."[4] So how do we live with the insecurity and uncertainty? By ourselves, we are probably incapable of handling the anxiety that comes with life.

All adults realize, on some level, either consciously or unconsciously, that we need a Higher Power. All of us, somewhere in our being, understand our frailty. Arrogance, however, deplores this awakening. Thus the arrogant person is not consciously aware of his need for a Higher Power.

Instead the arrogant person unconsciously chooses his savior. But unconscious decisions are decisions based on denial. This means making a choice before looking at one's choices. The arrogant person chooses a higher power without consciously acknowledging his need for such a force. Among things that these people worship are their egos, sanity, money, drugs and alcohol. They seek higher powers which they hope to control. They believe that once they control enough of this savior, they will become their own higher power. As a result, these people pursue their egos or money or alcohol until they become their own god. These addictions, however, never produce their desired ends.

A healthy approach to dealing with the anxiety inherent in life requires that the individual consciously choose one's higher power. This choice can only be made after one has developed a firm sense of humility. Only then can one consciously accept one's need for help.

A conscious search and struggle to know the Higher Power requires humility. Humility precedes spirituality. A humble person can strive to know God without trying to control Him. Humble people can live with the knowledge that there is more power in the universe than they can attain.

Some people deny the existence of God because they feel that God, if He existed, would not allow imperfection in the universe. But if we lived in a perfect world, we would have no control at all over our lives. There would be no risk, no challenge, no individuality. If everyone were gifted in all areas of our being, then no one would be unique. Our limitations help provide us with a sense of who we are. If we were all perfect, each of us would be identical and equally insignificant.

Instead we are given the opportunity to make something of ourselves (or not make something of ourselves). Because we do have some control of our lives we can take some pride in our accomplishments. We are given the potential to, partially, create ourselves. We are not given perfection. Rather, we are given potential. We are, in fact, given more potential than we can actualize in our limited lifespan.

I have always liked the adage, "Life is God's gift to you. What you do with your life is your gift to God." God may not give us perfection but I have never learned anything which indicates that He expects us to achieve perfection. Maybe the Hasidic rabbi Susya was correct when, shortly before his death, he said, "When I get to heaven they will not ask me, 'Why were you not Moses?' Instead they will ask, 'Why were you not Susya? Why did you not become what only you could become?' "[5]

If we are born with a mission, then the direction for our cause must lie in our unique arrangement of talents and limitations. Though we may scream for perfection, there is no evidence that God places this demand on us. We are born with a purpose. Part of our mission is finding that purpose. Our mission is not, however, to achieve perfection. Searching for perfection is like chasing a mirage. It wastes precious time.

When people think of God many of us think of perfection. But this does not necessarily improve their relationships with God. As I mentioned, some people foolishly believe that God represents perfection, and since we cannot see perfection in the universe there can be no God. Others feel that we cannot develop a relationship with God until we ourselves achieve perfection.

This latter belief is, in some ways, based on our childhood experiences. As children we learn that God lives in heaven—a place which epitomizes perfection. We also learn that we cannot get to this place until our souls are completely free of sin. These early encounters with the idea of God, no matter how simplistic, can have lasting effects. Many people, particularly people who feel inferior, refuse to believe that God would take the time to acknowledge their existence. This isolation can lead to deep despair.

Yet my clinical experience has shown me time and time again that this is precisely where many people find God—in the midst of deep despair. I have found that encounters with

God are most likely to occur following humbling experience.

Humility precedes spirituality. In other words, a person does not seek to encounter the spiritual dimension of his being until he has developed a healthy sense of humility. Once people stop fighting the limitations of our power, we can begin to recognize the power and majesty in our universe.

As we come to the end of this book we now look at what lies beyond the experience of humility. And what lies beyond humility is a larger, more complex universe. We are part of this universe. If we accept ourselves we can become one with the universe. If we cannot accept ourselves, we are at odds with the universe. We then feel alienated and become desperate for simple solutions.

We have discussed several of the most severe consequences of a life without humility. If we lack humility we will incur problems with our relationships and our self-esteem. We will not be able to work through grief or accept our own mortality. Without humility we cannot ask for help or express gratitude. Yet the most severe consequence of a life without humility is the way we restrict our lives.

People who never develop humility remain stuck in the physical and psychological dimensions of life. They are concerned only with the struggles they cannot possibly avoid. Primitive man may have been preoccupied with the fight for physical survival but modern man now focuses much more time on his emotional and psychological well-being. Because we are imperfect beings, we can spend our lifetimes analyzing the causes of our flaws.

Taking time for introspection can be time well spent. It can provide many important learning experiences. We should search ourselves to learn rather than perfect. Trying to perfect ourselves is an endless and fruitless mission which just keeps us from more important tasks.

If we can, on occasion, turn our attention away from ourselves we may hear a calling. This calling pulls us beyond ourselves, out of the restricted psychological world and into the limitless spiritual world. And, in spite of popular beliefs, our imperfect selves can learn a tremendous amount when we look well beyond ourselves.

Our cultural neglect of humility has indeed stifled our growth in numerous directions. But nowhere has this absence been felt more severely than in the realm of spirituality. If we accept ourselves, imperfect as we are, we can move beyond ourselves. And maybe then, somewhere off in the universe, we will get a glimpse at perfection.

Conclusion

I once met an artist in Boston who walked around the city and collected garbage. She then arranged the rubbish into wonderful works of art. I don't know how many people bought this art, but I do know that people liked to look at it. I think it made people think.

This artist never seemed to run out of garbage or ideas. She could use just about everything to make something. She mixed garbage and talent to create art.

When we integrate our limitations and our potential we discover new things about ourselves and our universe. What we are not and what we can never be compose a large part of who we are. If we can courageously and honestly face these limitations, we may find ourselves in the midst of a much greater and more secure universe.

FOOTNOTES

Introduction

1. Bill W., *The A.A. Way of Life: A Reader by Bill*. New York: Alcoholics Anonymous World Services, Inc.

Chapter One

1. Salloway, G., *Follow Me: Be Human*. Baltimore: Helicon, 1966.
2. Ibid. p 18.
3. Alcoholics Anonymous, *Twelve Steps and Twelve Traditions*. Alcoholics Anonymous World Services, Inc., p. 15.
4. Ibid. p. 71.
5. Maslow, A., *Motivation and Personality* (2nd Ed.). Harper and Row, 1970, p. 155.
6. Bill W., *The A.A. Way of Life: A Reader by Bill*. New York: Alcoholics Anonymous World Services, Inc.
7. Dresner, S.J., *Three Paths of God and Man*. New York: Harper and Brothers, 1960, p. 57.
8. Alcoholics Anonymous, *Twelve Steps and Twelve Traditions*. Alcoholics Anonymous World Services, Inc., p. 59.
9. Rogers, C., *On Becoming a Person*, Houghton Mifflin Company, 1961, p. 16.
10. Fromm, E., *To Have or To Be*, Harper and Row, 1976, p. 96.
11. Gaylin, W., *Feelings*, Ballantine Books, 1979, p. 77.
12. Mullaly, P., *The Beginnings of Modern American Psychiatry*. Boston: Houghton Mifflin Company, 1973.
13. Maslow, A., *Motivation and Personality* (2nd Ed.), Harper and Row, 1970, p. 45.
14. Ibid., p. 83.

Chapter Two

1. Dresner, S.H., *Three Paths of God and Man*. New York: Harper and Brothers, 1960, p. 59.
2. Goffman, E., *Stigma*, Prentice-Hall Inc., 1963, p. 128.
3. May, R., *Freedom and Destiny*, W.W. Norton and Co., 198_, p. 100.
4. Janoff-Bulman, R. and Frieze, I.H., "A theoretical perspective for understanding reactions to victimization." *Journal of Social Issues*, 39, 2, 1983.
5. Bill W., *The A.A. Way of Life: A Reader by Bill*. New York: Alcoholics Anonymous World Services, Inc.

Chapter Three

1. Yalom, Z., *Existential Psychotherapy*, Basic Books, 1980, p. 406.

Chapter Four

1. Heinrich, M.A., Price, S., Golden, J., "Transient Erectile Dysfunction," *Medical Aspects of Human Sexuality*, January, 1976.
2. May, R., *Freedom and Destiny*, W.W. Norton and Co., 1981, p. 242.
3. Ibid. p. 235.
4. Ibid. p. 347.
5. Schlossberg, N., Troll, L., Leibowitz, Z., *Perspectives on Counseling Adults: Issues and Skills*, Brooks/Cole Publishing Co., 1978, p. 19.
6. McCrae, R.R., "Age differences in the use of coping mechanisms," *Journal of Gerontology*, 37, 454-460, 1982.
7. Dresner, S.H., *Three Paths of God and Man*. New York: Harper and Brothers, 1960, p. 62.
8. Bill W., *The A.A. Way of Life: A Reader by Bill*. New York: Alcoholics Anonymous World Services, Inc., p. 139.
9. *Twelve Steps and Twelve Traditions*. New York: Alcoholics Anonymous World Services, Inc., p. 34.
10. Ibid. p. 76.

Chapter Five

1. Kubler-Ross, E., *On Death and Dying*, Macmillan Publishing Co. Inc., 1969, p. 113.
2. Cotter, F., *Coming to Terms with Death*, Nelson-Hall, 1974, p. 11.
3. Stair, N., "If I Had My Life To Live Over." Association for Humanistic Psychology Newsletter, July, 1975.
4. Bombeck, E., "What I Would Do . . . If I Had My Life To Live Over," *The Saturday Evning Post*, November, 1981, p. 16.
5. Raphael, B., *The Anatomy of Bereavement*, Basic Books, Inc., 1983, p. 401.

Chapter Six

1. *The Invisible Battle: Attitudes Toward Disability*, Regional Rehabilitation Research Institute on Attitudinal, Legal and Leisure Barriers, Washington, D.C.
2. Roessler, R. and Bolton, B., *Psychological Adjustment to Disability*, University Park Press, 1978, p. 19.
3. Ibid. p. 11.
4. Martin H., *The Abused Child*. Cambridge, Mass.: Ballinger, 1976.
5. Slater, P.E., *Pursuit of Loneliness: American Culture at the Breaking Point*. Boston: Beacon Press, 1970, p. 15.
6. Livneh, H., "On the Origins of Negative Attitudes toward People with Disabilities" in Marinelli, R.P. and Dell Orto, A.E. (Eds.), *The Psychological and Social Impact of Physical Disability*, Springer Publishing Co. Inc., 1984, p. 177.
7. Shontz, F.G., "Six Principles Relating Disability and Psychological Adjustment" in Marinelli, R.P. and Dell Orto, A.E. (Eds.), *The Psychological and Social Impact of Physical Disability*, Springer Publishing Co. Inc., 1984.

Chapter Seven

1. Buscaglia, L., *Love*, Fawcett Crest, 1972, p. 167.
2. I would like to thank Dr. Raphael J. Becvar of the Department of Education, St. Louis University for putting this idea in my head.
3. Rogers, C., *On Becoming a Person*, Houghton Mifflin Co., 1961, p. 16.
4. Fromm, E., *The Sane Society*, Fawcett Publications, 1955, p. 174.
5. Friedman, M., introduction to M. Buber, *Between Man and Man*. New York: Macmillan, 1965, p. xix.